Opening up Matthew's Gospel

IAIN D. CAMPBELL

DayOne

Opening up Matthew's Gospel ably combines careful attention to the text and structure of Matthew, sound theology, and insightful application. Concise and accessible without being superficial, this study of Matthew's Gospel commends itself to all levels of Christian readership. I warmly commend it.

—Guy Prentiss Waters, Associate Professor of New Testament, Reformed Theological Seminary, Jackson, Mississippi, USA

In *Opening up Matthew's Gospel,* Dr Iain D Campbell does precisely what the title of his latest book suggests with the clarity of a gifted preacher and the care of an able scholar. Dr Campbell leads the reader through the text of the Gospel, highlighting the most significant theological, historical and literary issues. Along the way, he draws on the insights of recent and older scholarship without allowing the reader to become swamped in technicalities or abstract debate. Concise but accurate exegesis, combined with some memorable expressions, will make this book popular with preachers. Probing questions at the end of each chapter serve to make this an excellent book for small study groups. I am glad to commend this book to all serious readers of Matthew.

—Rev. Dr Alistair I. Wilson, Principal, Dumisani Theological Institute, King William's Town, South Africa

Contents

First printed 2008

ISBN 978–1–84625–116–0

British Library Cataloguing in Publication Data available

Published by Day One Publications
Ryelands Road, Leominster, England, HR6 8NZ
Telephone 01568 613 740   FAX 01568 611 473

email—sales@dayone.co.uk
web site—www.dayone.co.uk
North American—e-mail-sales@dayonebookstore.com
North American web site—www.dayonebookstore.com

Printed by Gutenberg Press, Malta

To the pupils and staff of Special Class 1, Stornoway.

'You have hidden these things from the wise and understanding and revealed them to little children' (Matt. 11:25);

'You knitted me together in my mother's womb' (Ps. 139:13).

List of Bible abbreviations

THE OLD TESTAMENT

Gen.	Genesis
Exod.	Exodus
Lev.	Leviticus
Num.	Numbers
Deut.	Deuteronomy
Josh.	Joshua
Judg.	Judges
Ruth	Ruth
1 Sam.	1 Samuel
2 Sam.	2 Samuel
1 Kings	1 Kings
2 Kings	2 Kings
1 Chr.	1 Chronicles
2 Chr.	2 Chronicles
Ezra	Ezra
Neh.	Nehemiah
Esth.	Esther
Job	Job
Ps.	Psalms
Prov.	Proverbs
Eccles.	Ecclesiastes
S. of. S.	Song of Solomon
Isa.	Isaiah
Jer.	Jeremiah
Lam.	Lamentations
Ezek.	Ezekiel
Dan.	Daniel
Hosea	Hosea
Joel	Joel
Amos	Amos
Obad.	Obadiah
Jonah	Jonah
Micah	Micah
Nahum	Nahum
Hab.	Habakkuk
Zeph.	Zephaniah
Hag.	Haggai
Zech.	Zechariah
Mal.	Malachi

THE NEW TESTAMENT

Matt.	Matthew
Mark	Mark
Luke	Luke
John	John
Acts	Acts
Rom.	Romans
1 Cor.	1 Corinthians
2 Cor.	2 Corinthians
Gal.	Galatians
Eph.	Ephesians
Phil.	Philippians
Col.	Colossians
1 Thes.	1 Thessalonians
2 Thes.	2 Thessalonians
1 Tim.	1 Timothy
2 Tim.	2 Timothy
Titus	Titus
Philem.	Philemon
Heb.	Hebrews
James	James
1 Peter	1 Peter
2 Peter	2 Peter
1 John	1 John
2 John	2 John
3 John	3 John
Jude	Jude
Rev.	Revelation

Acknowledgements

I am grateful to Day One for the opportunity to contribute once again to the Opening Up series of Bible commentaries. I would like to thank them for publishing this manuscript, and to thank Jim Holmes and Suzanne Mitchell for their valuable work in preparing it for publication. I hope that it will enable people to read Matthew more meaningfully and to be and make good disciples for Jesus Christ.

Outline of Matthew's Gospel

Introduction—Behold your King!

Part 1—The King dwells among his people (1:1–4:16)

'Behold, your king is coming to you ...' (Zech. 9:9; Matt. 21:5)

Matthew introduces him

An angel announces him

Wise men seek him

Herod hunts him

John heralds him

God anoints him

Satan tempts him

Isaiah explains him

Part 2—The King declares his kingdom (4:17–16:20)

'Behold, your king is coming to you; righteous and having salvation is he ...' (Zech. 9:9)

The King's appeal: who will follow him? (4:17–25)

The King's speech: what is his kingdom like? (5–7)

- Portrait of blessedness
- Plea for righteousness
- Pattern for prayerfulness
- Promise of faithfulness
- Principles of holiness

The King's works: how does his kingdom advance? (8–9)

The King's followers: what is it like to serve him? (10–12)

- Commissioning the apostles
- Encouraging the herald
- The King as servant

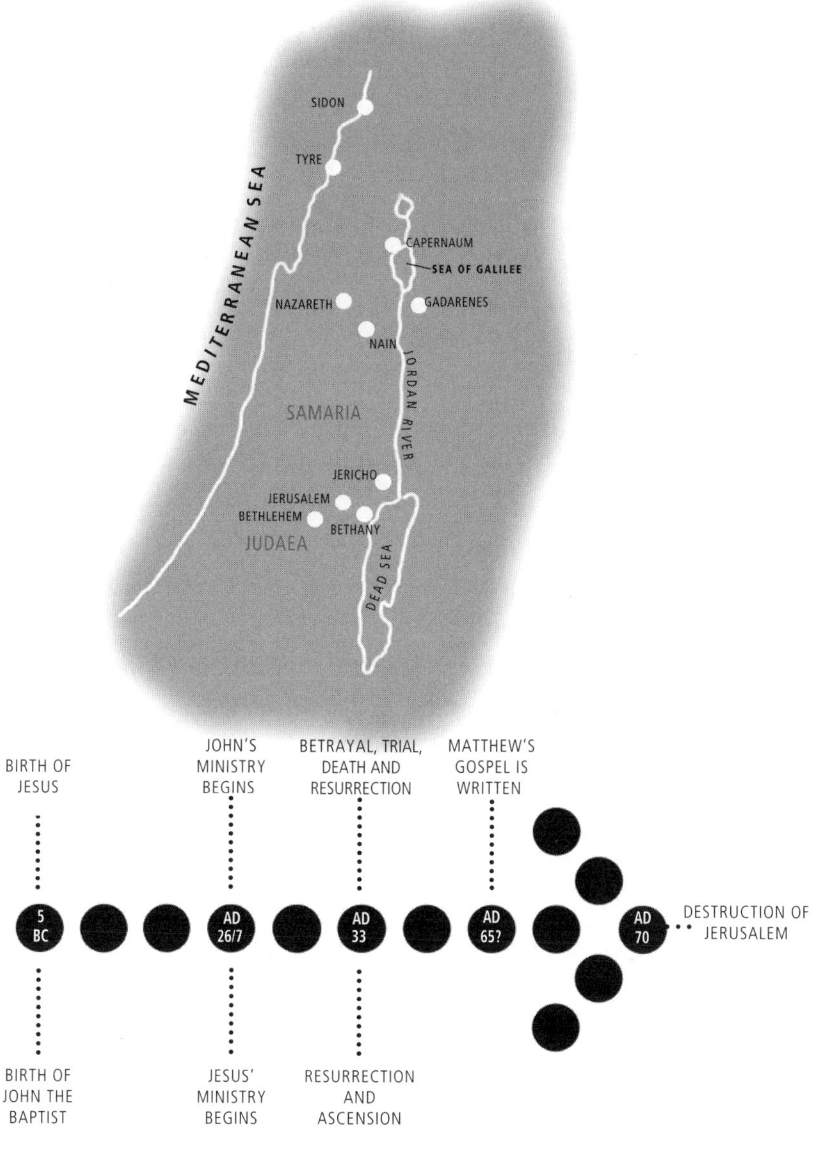

SIDON
TYRE
MEDITERRANEAN SEA
CAPERNAUM
SEA OF GALILEE
NAZARETH
GADARENES
NAIN
JORDAN RIVER
SAMARIA
JERICHO
JERUSALEM
BETHLEHEM
BETHANY
JUDAEA
DEAD SEA
BIRTH OF JESUS
JOHN'S MINISTRY BEGINS
BETRAYAL, TRIAL, DEATH AND RESURRECTION
MATTHEW'S GOSPEL IS WRITTEN
5 BC
AD 26/7
AD 33
AD 65?
AD 70
DESTRUCTION OF JERUSALEM
BIRTH OF JOHN THE BAPTIST
JESUS' MINISTRY BEGINS
RESURRECTION AND ASCENSION

Overview

Matthew, someone has said, followed Jesus—and took his pen with him. As a tax collector, he was used to writing and to gathering information together in a clear and ordered way. When Jesus called him to live the life of a disciple, Matthew (called Levi in other places) was destined to use his gifts to give us an ordered and carefully written account of who Jesus was and what he came to do.

As a disciple himself, Matthew focuses on three things: the King whom disciples follow, the lifestyle his disciples follow and the way in which people become disciples. The identification of Jesus as a king draws us back into the Old Testament, to themes and predictions which find their fulfilment in his life and work. Jesus' teaching, gathered by Matthew into five important teaching blocks, shows us what it means to be a follower and makes us ask ourselves whether we are following him.

Matthew's record was probably written not long before AD 70, the year the Romans sacked Jerusalem and destroyed the temple. It has become the first canonical Gospel: the entrance door into the New Testament, a link between the two parts of our Bible. Its opening verse reaches back to Abraham; its closing verse stretches forward to the end of the age. The story Matthew tells us about Jesus is timeless, as relevant to the church in the twenty-first century as it was in the first.

Maybe—just maybe—Matthew includes a veiled reference to himself in the words of Matthew 13:52: 'every scribe who has been trained for the kingdom of heaven is like a master of a house, who brings out of his treasure what is new and what is old.' Let's linger in Matthew's house and examine the treasure-box of the Gospel named after him.

Background & summary: Behold your King!

Why should we study Matthew's Gospel?

First, because of what it tells us about Jesus. This is the first of four records in the New Testament which follow the events of the life and work of Jesus Christ. They are all different, but they are all narrative records of Jesus' teaching and ministry. They focus partly on his early life, but mostly on his public ministry during the last three years of his life. Even then they spend much time on the closing days, which culminated in Jesus' death by crucifixion, then his glorious resurrection.

In particular, Matthew wants to emphasize three things about Jesus:

Jesus is our King

This emphasis is present from the very beginning, where Jesus is shown to be the son of David. He is the successor of David, the one in whom the promises of the covenant with David are fulfilled (2 Sam. 7:12). Though he was born in lowly circumstances and was deprived of much during his earthly life, he is still the King Matthew wants us to follow and serve.

Jesus is our Prophet

As our study will show, Matthew wants to make a comparison between Jesus and Moses, and show us that God's final revelation of his salvation and his purposes of grace for a fallen world is focused in Jesus Christ. This is a king who is also a prophet; in the words of one New Testament scholar, 'He wants to rule the world, not by troops but by words.'[1] Or, in the words of Matthew's record, God says to us of Jesus, 'This is my beloved Son, with whom I am well pleased; listen to him' (Matt. 17:5).

The similarities between Jesus and Moses are striking. As we shall see in the commentary, there are five main teaching blocks in this Gospel (chs. 5–7, 10, 13, 18 and 24–25). These may correspond to the five books of Moses. There are also references to mountains, where Jesus teaches and where his glory is displayed; these echo parts of the narrative sections of the Book of Exodus, where Moses appears. Moses predicted the coming of a prophet like himself (Deut. 18:15–19); Matthew wants us to know that he has finally come.

> Matthew's unmistakeable emphasis is that this Person, and this Person alone, is able to help us recover from the tragedy of our unbelief and estrangement from God.

Jesus is our Saviour

His name, highlighted at the beginning of the Gospel, means that he saves his people from their sins (Matt. 1:21). His death is not a tragic loss; it represents the shedding of his blood for our forgiveness (Matt. 26:28). Matthew's unmistakeable emphasis is that this Person, and this Person alone, is able to help us recover from the tragedy of our unbelief and estrangement from God.

Second, we should study Matthew because of what this Gospel tells us about discipleship. Matthew was a disciple and his Gospel is about discipleship. It is about hearing the call of Jesus, not just the voice of Jesus. It is about living the life of a disciple, a follower of Jesus.

Indeed, Matthew features in his own story, albeit very briefly, at Matthew 9:9 (and again, even more briefly, at Matthew 10:3). He probably had his own reasons for not spending more time on autobiographical detail, but we know that our author had himself heard the call to discipleship, had got up and followed Jesus. He had been a tax-collector, recording the payment of taxes to the Romans, but Jesus had a different use for his pen. His Gospel was probably written just before AD 70, and more than likely he borrowed from Mark. The comment of Matthew-scholar Craig Keener rings true: 'Matthew did not write his Gospel without forethought ... Like other writers, Matthew would follow one main source (in this case Mark) and weave his other sources around it.'[2]

Certainly by the time Eusebius wrote his *Ecclesiastical History* in the third century, the writings of Matthew were regarded as canonical. Eusebius quoted Papias (who died about AD 135), who spoke about 'the words of the elders—what Andrew or what Peter said, or what was said by Philip, or by Thomas, or by James, or by John, or by Matthew'.[3] Matthew's credentials were not in doubt; he was a disciple, writing for disciples about discipleship.

That is why the Gospel concludes with the commission to the disciples to make more disciples (Matt. 28:16–20). The Gospel record of the life of Jesus is the foundation for the ongoing work of the followers of Christ, who long to see others enrolled in his service and dedicating their lives to him. Through parables, benedictions and teachings, Matthew shows us the blessings of being the disciples of Jesus.

> The Gospel record of the life of Jesus is the foundation for the ongoing work of the followers of Christ, who long to see others enrolled in his service and dedicating their lives to him.

This resonates with Matthew's emphasis on the kingdom. We need to know the King, but we also need to know about the kingdom over which he is sovereign. The kingdom is the constituency he has called into his service. It is a spiritual kingdom, made up of those whose lives he has transformed by his saving work.

For this reason, Matthew emphasizes the importance of the church. His Gospel highlights the relationship between the kingdom of God (or the kingdom of heaven) and the church. God's kingdom includes all those in heaven and earth who confess him and worship him as their God. That comes to expression in the world in the church, the called-out and yet ingathered company of his people, who love to worship him, in whose company he wants to be present, and whose goal is to honour him and support one another (see Matt. 18:15–20).

Third, we should study Matthew because of the encouragement his Gospel gives us to preach the Good News. We not only honour Jesus and make disciples, we also have a reason to preach the gospel. Not only has Jesus commissioned us to go out with the news of salvation, but his own death and resurrection give us the sole reason for persevering in that task.

At the beginning of his story, Matthew records wise men coming to Jesus from far away (Matt. 2:1–12); at the end, Matthew records Jesus sending his disciples far away to bring Jesus to men. For the readers of Matthew's Gospel, the story of Jesus doesn't end. It keeps going, until it reaches its great culmination in his second coming. That's our horizon.

Let's study Matthew's story, to see the reason why.

Part 1—The King dwells among his people

(1:1–4:16)

'Behold, your king is coming to you …'
(Zech. 9:9; Matt. 21:5)

1 The King appears

(1:1–2:23)

Matthew's Gospel does not begin with a straightforward introduction: it begins with a genealogy, a description of the ancestors of Jesus. It seems a strange way to start a story, but it is an extremely important way of leading into the most important story ever told.

Matthew introduces the King (1:1–17)

The genealogy of Jesus is given in the opening verses of the Gospel, with an introductory verse summarizing that Jesus is 'the son of David, the son of Abraham'.

It may seem strange that Matthew should open his Gospel with this kind of introduction. But the genealogy serves to do several things. First, it anchors the whole message of this Gospel in Old Testament history. We begin, not with Jesus, but with Abraham. To understand Jesus, we need the Old Testament, just as to understand the Old Testament, we need Jesus. The history is redemptive and anticipates the coming of Jesus Christ.

Second, the genealogy witnesses to the genuine humanity of the Saviour. He has ancestors and relations. There is a bloodline which runs all the way from Abraham to him. He came down from heaven, but it is among men that he appears, on earth, as part of our race. He is God and he is man.

Third, the genealogy serves to legitimize Christ's exclusive claims. He speaks as a king because he is the King. He is heir to David's crown. God promised Abraham that kings would come from him (Gen. 17:6), and promised David that his throne would be established for ever (2 Sam. 7:16). Now the King has appeared.

The genealogy is divided by Matthew into three parts. The first takes us from Abraham to David and illustrates *God's sovereign grace* in the world. What else could account for the call of Abraham, or the salvation of Judah, or the inclusion of Tamar and Ruth in this genealogy? Why should our Saviour have Gentile blood in his veins? The answer is, because of the great grace of God, which was working on the theatre of the world's history; and the more we think of it, the more we cry out, 'Oh, the depth of the riches and wisdom and knowledge of God! How unsearchable are his judgements and how inscrutable his ways!' (Rom. 11:33).

The second part runs from David to the exile in Babylon and illustrates *God's singular purpose* in Old Testament history. The names in the second part of the genealogy are all of kings of Judah. Some are omitted, although this abbreviated version is still a remarkable testimony to the way in which the bloodline of Christ ran through the successive kings of the southern kingdom. Although Judah's history witnessed spiritual degeneration resulting in exile, God was still preserving a royal seed in succession to David and which looked forward to the coming of Jesus Christ.

The third part runs from the exile to Jesus and illustrates *God's saving work* in the world. Just as the redemptive history opened with redemption from Egypt, so it closes with salvation from Babylon and restoration to the land of promise. God did not abandon his people but worked to bring them back.

The stage is now set. We know who the King is. But how will he appear?

An angel announces the King (1:18–25)

The royal theme is continued with the announcement by a heavenly messenger that the King is coming. Matthew tells the story from Joseph's point of view (unlike Luke, who tells it from the point of view of Mary). Joseph, a carpenter from Nazareth, is 'betrothed' (formally engaged) to Mary. Matthew's version of the story is that Mary falls pregnant through a special act of the Holy Spirit; Joseph, who wants to avoid the public scandal to which this situation might lead, decides to make private arrangements for the engagement to be annulled.

Both the reality and the supernatural nature of Jesus' conception are highlighted in Matthew's account. The incarnation was nothing other than the real 'enfleshment' of the Son of God—Jesus took our human nature and entered into our world through the door of the virginal conception. Mary was Jesus' natural mother, but Jesus had no human father. The ministry of the Holy Spirit, which will be an important motif in Matthew's Gospel, is highlighted first in relation to the incarnation of Jesus.

Both the reality and the supernatural nature of Jesus' conception are highlighted in Matthew's account. The incarnation was nothing other than the real 'enfleshment' of the Son of God—Jesus took our human nature and entered into our world through the door of the virginal conception.

Jesus grew up under the scandal of Mary's alleged immorality. On one occasion, the Jewish leaders threw at him the comment that they were not the product of sexual immorality, as they considered him to be (John 8:41). But the Holy Spirit, who had at the beginning hovered over the darkness to effect the creation of the universe, enshrouded the darkness of Mary's womb to effect the creation of the human nature of our Lord.

The announcement to Joseph is made by an 'angel' (v. 20). The ministry of the angels in the Word of God is important, not least in the record of the life of Christ. Angels witness both to his birth and to his resurrection (see 28:2–7). The angel's message highlights several things. First, it is God's will that Joseph should marry Mary. Second, the pregnancy is supernatural, mysterious and miraculous, the work of the Holy Spirit. Third, the baby will be male. Fourth, the name of their son will be 'Jesus' (this was a common name related to 'Joshua', the name of Moses' successor who led God's people into the land of Canaan). Fifth, in connection with his name, this child is to save his people.

This was an unexpected announcement indeed. Yet, as Matthew tells us, it was nothing other than the fulfilment of Isaiah's prophecy that 'the virgin shall conceive and bear a son, and shall call his name Immanuel' (Isa. 7:14). 'Immanuel' means 'God with us', and finds its echo in Jesus' promise at the very end of the Gospel: 'I am with you always' (28:20). Matthew also tells us that Joseph and Mary had no sexual relations until after the birth of Jesus.

Wise men seek the King (2:1–12)

The visit of the wise men from the east has always been an intriguing part of the Jesus story. In popular culture we have developed the idea of 'three kings from the Orient', but there is no indication that they held such high office. The significance of their appearance is twofold: they follow a strange star all the way to Bethlehem, where Jesus was born, and they come from far away to worship him.

The first of these facts has led to a great deal of speculation. Were they astronomers? Or astrologers? What led them to recognize the significance of this star so as to follow it all this way? Phil Ryken surmises that the wise men 'witnessed several conjunctions of Jupiter, the planet they considered to represent kingship'.[1] But more important, he argues, is the theological meaning of this: 'From the very creation of the world, God organized the solar system—and indeed the entire universe—in a way that would signify the birth of his Son and our Saviour, Jesus Christ.'[2]

The second fact is equally significant: these wise men come from afar to worship Jesus. That itself is remarkable, but in the context of Matthew's Gospel it is supremely important, because the church is commissioned to go into all the world with the gospel (28:19). The fact that the world comes to Jesus in the first place is a wonderful indication of the universal significance that his birth is to have.

Herod hunts the King (2:13–23)

If there are wise men on the scene, there are foolish men around, too. Herod belongs to the latter group. The dynasty of Herods who ruled Judea in the time of Christ began with Herod the Great (usually dated as ruler from 37 to 4 BC). Politically, Herod was a successful ruler; but his spiritual condition is evident when the wise men appear correctly citing Micah 5:2 as a prophecy that the messianic King will come from Bethlehem.

Herod tries to locate Jesus but fails to do so. God takes steps to ensure that he and the wise men will not meet again.

The wise men find Jesus and worship him in the house (note that 2:11 does not say that they went into the stable). They present gifts of gold (suitable for a king), frankincense (suitable for a priest) and myrrh (a symbol of suffering and death that appears in John 19:39 as an ingredient in the burial of Jesus). What they know of the significance of these gifts is not told us; they simply offer them in an act of worship.

Meanwhile, Herod is scheming to prevent the prophecy of Micah going any further. Having learned that the wise men have returned home, he takes matters into his own hands and slaughters all the infants under two years of age in Bethlehem and round about. This slaughter is another fulfilment of Old Testament prophecy (Jer. 31:15).

The safety of Jesus is guaranteed by God himself. He declares to Joseph by his angel that he must take Jesus to Egypt (2:13). He will be safe there. And he will be identified there with the exodus redemption of the Old Testament, a point made explicit by the citation in 2:15 of Hosea 11:1, where the declaration that God's Son (Israel) was taken safely out of Egypt finds its ultimate meaning in the historical fact that God's Son (Jesus) was also taken safely out of Egypt. Matthew wants us to see Jesus' life and ministry in terms of redemption and salvation, continuing the redemptive history of the Old Testament.

After the death of Herod, an angelic announcement allows the holy family to return to Israel, to Nazareth, where Jesus will grow up. Matthew tells us that this fulfilled the prophecy that he would be a Nazarene, although there is no verse which corresponds exactly to this. There could be a reference here to the Hebrew word *nezer* (meaning 'a branch') which is used of the Messiah in Isaiah 11:1; there could also be a reference to the Nazirite vow under which Samson the judge of Israel was placed (Judg. 13:7) since, like Samson, Jesus was consecrated to God as the deliverer of his people.

FOR FURTHER STUDY

1. Matthew describes Jesus as the 'son of Abraham' and the 'son of David' (1:1). How do the following passages link in to these themes: Acts 2:30–31; Romans 1:3–4; Galatians 3:16; Revelation 22:16?
2. There is a reference to the Holy Spirit in Matthew 1:18. What is the reference? In which other contexts does Matthew mention the Holy Spirit?
3. In 1:23, Matthew quotes Isaiah 7:14. What is the purpose of the quotation? Was God with his people in Old Testament times? How is he with us today?
4. Compare the words of Matthew 2:15 with the original quotation in Hosea 11:1. Who is the 'son' in Hosea? And in Matthew?

TO THINK ABOUT AND DISCUSS

1. What do you understand by the 'virgin birth of Jesus Christ'? How important is this for our Christian faith?
2. Matthew 1:21 tells us that the name 'Jesus' is linked with salvation from sin. How does Jesus save us?
3. Why does Matthew quote so often from the Old Testament? How can the Old Testament help us better understand who Jesus is and why Jesus came?
4. Why do you think we are told so little about Jesus' early life and development?

2 The King begins his ministry

(Matthew 3:1–4:17)

The beginnings of Jesus' public ministry are described in chapters 3 and 4. Matthew has not spent much time on the infancy narrative—just enough to remind us that Jesus was no ordinary Jewish boy; he was God's Saviour, God himself with us. Now this great Saviour was going to stride across the stage of history in a public way.

John heralds the King (3:1–12)

In 3:1 we are introduced to John the Baptist, who will make further appearances in chapters 11 and 14. John appears preaching the gospel of the kingdom and calling his hearers to repentance. This introduces the theme of Jesus' ministry also (compare 4:17). Isaiah had predicted the appearance of a forerunner, one who would announce beforehand the coming Lord. Later, Jesus would also identify John with Elijah (17:12–13).

Like Elijah, John's appearance is rough and unattractive. But his message is listened to, and many come to him repenting of their sins and being baptized in the Jordan. Although we meet him in the first of the New Testament Gospels, John was, in many ways, the last of the Old Testament prophets and his ministry was very much in Old Testament language and terms.

His ministry was also particularly aimed at the religious leaders, the Pharisees and the Sadducees. Merrill Tenney described the Pharisees as 'the separatists, or Puritans of Judaism'.[1] Many, but not all, were concerned merely with external observance of religion. Saul of Tarsus, later the leading Gentile missionary of the early church, called himself 'a Pharisee, a son of Pharisees' (Acts 23:6) and considered himself blameless before God through his observance of God's law (Phil. 3:6). Much of Jesus' teaching in the Sermon on the Mount was directed at the Pharisees. The Sadducees were the descendants of Zadok, who was high priest in the days of Solomon. They, too, adhered to the Law, but they were anti-supernaturalists and denied the resurrection.

John did not mince his words, describing the religious leaders as 'a brood of vipers' for whom the judgement of God was prepared (v. 7). Jesus was portrayed as the one who would 'baptize [them] with the Holy Spirit and fire', a reference to his dual function as Saviour and Judge. These are themes Matthew will explore later in his Gospel. This uncompromising ministry would eventually lead to John's execution.

God anoints the King (3:13–17)

Parallel passages for the baptism narrative are found in Mark 1:9–11; Luke 3:21–22; and John 1:32–34. Here, the baptism has a twofold literary function. First, it provides a two-part introduction to Jesus' messianic ministry, emphasizing both the *content* and the *place* of his ministry. Jesus will proclaim, 'Repent, for the kingdom of heaven is at hand' (Matt. 4:17). It is fitting, therefore, that he should identify himself with the baptism of repentance, which involves both the voice and the descent of the Spirit from heaven. That beginning of ministry, however, is marked by Matthew in the following way: in Matthew 3:13, Jesus comes *from* Galilee, and in 4:12, he returns *to* Galilee. This is where—in order to fulfil Old Testament prophecy—the declaration of the Good News should begin.

But there is a second reason why the baptism is important in Matthew. For the first evangelist, there is an intimate correlation between the work of Jesus and the ongoing work of the church. Just as the Father has sent him, so he sends us (see John 20:21). The mission of Jesus begins in a public way with his baptism and it ends with the commission which he leaves to his church to fulfil after him, recorded in the closing verses of Matthew's Gospel.

There, in the Great Commission, baptism is central and significant: 'Go therefore and make disciples of all nations, baptizing them in the name of the Father and of the Son and of the Holy Spirit' (Matt. 28:19). In addition, the Great Commission contains the promise of Christ's presence.

The Christian name of God is a triune name: 'Father and

… Son and … Holy Spirit'. These three persons of the Godhead are each involved in this significant moment of the anointing of Jesus:

God the Father: heard but not seen

A voice speaks from heaven. It is the voice of the Father of the One who is being baptized. Immediately, therefore, we are confronted with the reality that the Father of this Son is in heaven, while the Son of this Father is on earth. Jesus is already the Son of this Father. God is his Father, not by adoption but by nature. This Son was with the Father but is distinct from the Father, even as, to borrow from John 1:1, he was with God and was God.

The voice of the Father registers his delight in all that the Son does. Like Wisdom, exulting in the knowledge of being daily the delight of God (Prov. 8:30), the Son is the constant delight of the Father. In the Son the Father is well pleased. The Son has the Father's approval from the outset. In the drama of this baptism is made explicit what Isaiah reveals but sees so very dimly: that God says of God, 'Behold my servant, whom I uphold, my chosen, in whom my soul delights' (Isa. 42:1).

God the Holy Spirit: seen but not heard

Isaiah said more, of course. The one who delights in his servant also says, 'I have put my Spirit upon him' (Isa. 42:1). So now, at the baptism of Jesus, the Spirit of God descends like a dove to rest on Jesus. Matthew has already drawn our attention to the intimate relationship between Jesus Christ and the Holy Spirit. The virginal conception of Jesus was by the power of the Holy Spirit (Matt. 1:20). The mission of Jesus is to be understood in terms of Jesus' baptizing his people with the Holy Spirit (Matt. 3:11).

And now, the Spirit-filled Jesus, who will impart the Spirit to others, receives the Holy Spirit himself in a fresh anointing that marks both the commencement of his public ministry and the Father's equipping of Jesus for that ministry.

Matthew records that a dove is seen (compare John 1:32) but he knows it to be the Holy Spirit. Interestingly, he makes Jesus the subject of the verb: '*he* saw the Spirit of God descending' (3:16). Jesus knew what this was and who this was. And it was part of his complete acquiescence in the Father's will that he should receive this new filling of the Spirit for the task ahead. The reception of the Holy Spirit on his part was a means to an end: that he might fulfil the will of the Father.

God the Son: seen and heard

The striking thing about all of this is that it took the enfleshment of one person of the Godhead to reveal the whole Trinity to us. It is because Jesus was where he was, in our nature and identified with his people, that we now enjoy this enlarged revelation of God. 'While only the Son became man, the Incarnation nevertheless reveals the whole Trinity.'[2]

So here is Jesus, at the beginning of his ministry as at its close, numbered among the transgressors, not ashamed to call them his brothers and placing himself under the law to redeem those who are under the law. A trinity of condescension, love and grace combine in this moment of theophany as the God-man, clothes dripping from his standing in Jordan's streams, receives a shower of blessing from on high.

Satan tempts the King (4:1–11)

Remarkably, from the heights of baptism blessing Jesus descends into wilderness temptation. It is not accidental—the same Spirit who anointed him in chapter 3 leads him into the wilderness to be tempted. The fasting for forty days and forty nights is another link to the past: Israel, redeemed from Egypt, spent forty years in the wilderness 'tested' by the word of God (see Deut. 8:2). Now Jesus, called out of Egypt, also spends his probation in the wilderness.

> The striking thing about all of this is that it took the enfleshment of one person of the Godhead to reveal the whole Trinity to us. It is because Jesus was where he was, in our nature and identified with his people, that we now enjoy this enlarged revelation of God.

But there are deeper associations here. After all, sin entered the world by temptation in a garden. Adam failed the probation, and sin passed into all men. Now Jesus is tempted in a wilderness. He will stand where Adam fell, and will bring salvation into human experience. For this reason, says the writer to the Hebrews, it was fitting that Jesus should be tempted: 'Therefore he had to be made like his brothers in every respect, so that he might become a merciful and faithful high priest in the service of God, to make propitiation for the sins of the people. For because he himself has suffered when tempted, he is able to help those who are being tempted' (Heb. 2:17–18).

The reality of the temptation is not diminished by the fact that Jesus has no sin and cannot sin. He feels its full force and has to resist until the tempter withdraws from him. Satan takes advantage of Jesus' location (the isolation of the wilderness) and of Jesus' condition (he is hungry), but he cannot bring him to yield.

The temptations focus in a particular way on the deity of Christ. The voice at the baptism declared him to be the Son of God; the voice in the wilderness now says, 'If you are the Son of God …' In the first assault, the devil wants Jesus to perform a miracle in order to meet his physical need; in the second, he wants him to throw himself from the pinnacle of the temple in order to test whether God will keep his promise; in the third, he wants him to obtain what God has promised him (all the kingdoms of the world) by the devil's way, avoiding the cross altogether.

Jesus' resource for meeting these assaults is the Word of God. Interestingly, he finds the Book of Deuteronomy particularly appropriate; and that should not surprise us, since it was given to Israel in the Old Testament. Now, for the true Israel, in the wilderness for his people, the ancient Word of God is the only adequate help.

One angel—the devil—recedes, while other angels minister to him.

Isaiah explains the King (4:12–17)

The stage is now set for the public ministry of Jesus to begin in earnest. Following the arrest of John the Baptist, Jesus begins his own ministry in the territory of Zebulun and Naphtali, in the region of Capernaum. Isaiah had said as much of the Messiah, as the quotation in verses 15–16 from Isaiah 9:1–2 demonstrates.

Now Matthew includes the first of two important markers for the ministry of Jesus by telling us that '*From that time* Jesus began to preach ...' (4:17). The focus of the Gospel is not going to be on general biography but on the last three years of Jesus' life, the years in which he was set apart as the Messenger of the Covenant, the King who declared that the kingdom of heaven was breaking into the experience of men and women.

For further study ▶

FOR FURTHER STUDY

1. While Matthew simply records that 'John the Baptist came preaching in the wilderness' (3:1), Luke records more details about the birth of John. Read Luke 1 and see what similarities you can find between the births of John and Jesus.
2. Read 2 Kings 1:8. About whom is the author of 2 Kings writing? Where do these details appear in Matthew's story? What is the significance of this?
3. Matthew 3:10 talks about trees bearing fruit. Can you find a similar reference elsewhere in Matthew? What do the following passages tell us about the importance of bearing fruit: Psalm 92:14; Hosea 14:8; John 15:1–5; Galatians 5:22–23?
4. Jesus quotes from Deuteronomy as he answers the devil in Matthew 4:4,7,10. However, there are other allusions to Deuteronomy in the passage. Compare 4:1 with Deuteronomy 8:2, and 4:2 with Deuteronomy 9:9. How might we compare Jesus with Israel?
5. How do Hebrews 2:18 and 4:15 shed light on the significance of Jesus' temptations?

TO THINK ABOUT AND DISCUSS

1. What was the point of John the Baptist's ministry? Can we draw any lessons about preaching from the way in which he delivered his message?
2. There have been two different approaches to baptism in the Christian church, with some arguing that only believers should be baptized and others arguing that the covenant children of believers may also be baptized. On what basis is each position adopted? Do you consider one to be more scriptural than the other? Is this issue important enough for believers to divide from one another?
3. How does the doctrine of the Trinity impact your reading of the Bible? Your approach to worship?
4. Are you aware of the devil tempting you? What are your weaknesses? Do you find it easy to resist temptation?

Part 2—The King declares his kingdom

(4:17–16:20)

'Behold, your king is coming to you; righteous and having salvation is he …' (Zech. 9:9)

3 The King convenes his parliament

(4:17–7:29)

The King-Prophet now begins to teach his disciples. His words will cut across the hypocrisy and formalism of many of the current religious leaders. He will lay down challenges to his people, all the time encouraging them to build their lives on the sure foundation of his own teaching.

The King's appeal: who will follow him? (4:17–25)

The beginning of this record of Jesus' ministry is marked by a note about those who followed him. Two sets of brothers are called by Jesus and become the first disciples. They are Simon Peter and Andrew, followed by James and John. The fact that Peter is named first is probably an indication of the important roles he will have later, both within this Gospel and in relation to the Christian church and its mission.

The first call to discipleship is to fishermen, whose work is now to be 'fishers of men'. In fact, Jesus' ministry will involve him going out in a boat with these men of the sea (8:23–27) and will also include stories and parables centred around the occupation of the fishermen (see, for example, 13:47–48).

But, in addition to the special call of the disciples, the ministry of Jesus appeals to a wider audience. As he teaches throughout Galilee and heals the sick, 'great crowds followed him' (4:25). This section forms an important bridge to the 'Sermon on the Mount'; 'Seeing the crowds' (5:1), Jesus goes up onto a mountain.

The King's speech: what is his kingdom like? (5:1–7:29)

The Sermon on the Mount is the first of the five sections of teaching in Matthew's Gospel and is really a statement of life within God's kingdom. I often compare it to the Queen's Speech at the State Opening of Parliament. Each November in the United Kingdom, when the new session of Parliament officially begins, the monarch reads a speech outlining the policies which his or her government will pursue over the coming year. Amid great pomp and ceremony, with many theatrical touches, the Queen's Speech is a statement of intent, declaring a programme of government.

There is no pomp or ceremony in the Sermon on the Mount. But there are echoes of the Old Testament; we are meant, perhaps, to see Jesus as the new Moses, outlining the rule of God in the lives of members of his new community. This is the formal inauguration of his kingdom; here the King sets out his plan, the programme by which his kingdom is identified and his rule administered.

So what do we have in the Sermon on the Mount?

Portrait of Blessedness (5:2–16)

The first theme we find is a description of the character of those who belong to the kingdom of Jesus Christ. Before we come to hear his standards, we stand before this portrait of his subjects. This passage, in which Jesus describes his followers as 'Blessed', is known as the 'Beatitudes' (from the Latin word for blessing).

It is important to note that the Sermon on the Mount is *descriptive* before it is *prescriptive*. It describes what the Christian *is* before talking of what the Christian *should do*. For Jesus, obedience grows out of blessedness; the statement of our condition precedes the demands of our discipleship. All the imperatives of the gospel arise out of its indicatives.

In each of these benedictions there is a description of character followed by an explanation of what makes such people 'blessed'. God's people are 'poor in spirit' (v. 3), meaning that they acknowledge their spiritual bankruptcy and their need of the grace of the kingdom. They are in a world of sorrow, in which they 'mourn' (v. 4). They are 'meek' (v. 5), not boastful or arrogant. They 'hunger and thirst for righteousness' (v. 6), meaning that they long both to be and to do what is right and just. They are 'merciful' (v. 7), living in response to the mercy of God shown to them. They are 'pure in heart' (v. 8), living under the light of gospel forgiveness and gospel holiness. They are 'peacemakers' (v. 9), lovers of peace and makers of peace. And they are persecuted for the sake of what is right (vv. 10–11), reviled for the truth, just as the prophets were.

To list these characteristics is to be aware of two things: first, that the kingdom of Jesus Christ is a kingdom of the heart. Yes, it is a real kingdom, and Jesus is a real king. But the life of the kingdom is principally a spiritual life, a matter of the heart; and it has to be a matter of the heart before it can become anything else.

Second, life in the kingdom can be hard. Jesus does not call his people to follow him with the promise of unbounded wealth or perfect health. He does promise blessings, but sometimes they will be experienced in the pain of rejection and loss.

However, to be 'blessed' means to relate to God in a particular way. Some modern translations substitute the word 'happy' for the word 'blessed' and make the whole thing into a feeling. But Jesus is not talking about our feelings in this passage. As John Stott says, 'Happiness is a subjective state, whereas Jesus is making an objective judgement about these people.'[1] This is what God says about them. It is to those who have nothing in themselves that God gives the kingdom of heaven, the comfort of heaven, the earth as their inheritance, the satisfaction of his provision, the mercy and vision of God, the right to be called his sons and the greatest of all rewards: a place in his kingdom.

This is the very opposite of a worldly outlook. Jesus is promising the greatest of all blessings to those who are part of his kingdom. These are blessings both for the present and for the future. And they are blessings of usefulness, for those whose lives are portrayed here are the salt of the earth (v. 13) and the light of the world (v. 14). They are in a position of influence and good in which they are able to stem the tide of corruption and darkness that engulfs a fallen world.

Plea for righteousness (5:17–48)

Two recurring themes run through the Sermon on the Mount and they are encapsulated for us in the words Jesus uses. In 5:17 Jesus says, 'I have not come to abolish [the Law and the Prophets]'; and in 5:22, 28, 32, 34 and 44 he uses the phrase 'But I say to you'.

These parallel themes help us to understand what Jesus is doing in the Sermon on the Mount. On the one hand, he is preserving, continuing and fulfilling what God had previously revealed in the Old Testament. His function was not to 'abolish' either the Law or the Prophets; rather, Jesus saw himself as standing in that same stream of revelation, his teachings being of a piece with what the Old Testament had declared.

That does not mean that everything was to continue as it was before. By fulfilling the Law, some aspects of Old Testament legislation were to be rendered obsolete. For example, the sacrifices and ceremonies associated with redemption and atonement were, in fact, to be done away with because Jesus came to fulfil them and to usher in perfect righteousness. Much of the letter to the Hebrews is taken up with precisely that theme.

On the other hand, extracting the true meaning of Old Testament law meant a break with the received Jewish, rabbinical teaching of the day. So when Jesus says, 'But I say to you', he is not setting himself over against Moses, but over against those whose interpretations of the Law had turned

God's covenant of grace into a covenant of works. For too many people, righteousness was a matter of obeying all the rules; no, says Jesus, the rules require us to go deeper than the shallow religion of the rabbis might suggest.

This is what Jesus means when he says that 'unless your righteousness exceeds that of the scribes and Pharisees, you will never enter the kingdom of heaven' (v. 20). Belonging to his kingdom, and living the kingdom life, takes more than external conformity to a set of religious standards. It has to go deeper than that.

Jesus illustrates this with reference to six practical issues. The first has to do with the meaning of the prohibition of *murder* (vv. 21–26). The commandment was clear: 'You shall not murder.' The Pharisees and scribes understood this in its narrowest sense, believing that if they had never shed innocent blood, they had kept the commandment. But Jesus says that the commandment extends to 'emotional murder', to a sense of resentment and anger against someone. Such anger is itself a violation on man made in the image of God. God cannot accept our offering if we are angry with our brother (vv. 23–24).

The second has to do with the commandment on *adultery* (vv. 27–30). Again, there were those who prided themselves on the fact that they had never committed adultery simply because they had never carried through the physical act of sleeping with another woman. But Jesus says that our righteousness has to go deeper than this. Adultery does not begin in the bed, but in the heart. What about the lust factor in our lives? That's where the sin is committed and where its influence must be dealt with and cut off.

The third is in the area of *divorce* (vv. 31–32), a subject taken up again by Jesus in chapter 19. While the rabbis were arguing over whether divorce could be allowed in certain situations, Jesus was much more concerned to defend the creation ordinance of marriage against those who trivialized it. The summary statement in the Sermon on the Mount is a clear indication of the high value Jesus places on marriage.

The fourth area is that of *religious oaths* (vv. 33–37). The Old Testament emphasized that God hated a false oath (Zech. 8:17) and that 'It is better that you should not vow than that you should vow and not pay' (Eccles. 5:5). To safeguard themselves in this matter, the Pharisees had devised elaborate formulae and were satisfied that these guarded their integrity. Whatever they vowed was pure, and the purity was safeguarded by the right formula (swearing 'by the earth' or 'by Jerusalem'—v. 35). If, however, the oath was not kept, they could claim that they had not invoked the name of God and were therefore blameless. Jesus cuts through the hypocrisy of this and calls for integrity in all our speech.

The fifth area is that of *retaliation* (vv. 38–42). The principle of giving 'an eye for an eye' (known as the *lex talionis*) was part of the Old Testament case law which provided safeguards against damage to personal property and possessions. The problem was that the rabbis of Jesus' day were misusing this provision of the Law; they had 'extended this principle of just retribution from the law courts (where it belongs) to the realm of personal relationships (where it does not belong)'.[2] They justified retaliation and the taking of revenge by a law that was designed to prevent just that. There are occasions when we must endure wrongful suffering (1 Peter 2:20). Jesus' words are not a call to absolute pacifism but to submission to God in every circumstance.[3]

Finally, Jesus deals with the topic of *love for our enemies* (vv. 43–48). The rabbis justified their attitude to Gentiles on the basis of passages in the Old Testament whose meanings were hidden away under layers of interpretation and addition. Jesus, however, cuts the ground from under any form of discrimination, citing as his authority the common goodness and grace of God, who makes the rain to fall and the sun to rise on both the evil and the good. It is the standard of our heavenly Father we are to reach, and it is his example we are to follow.

Pattern for prayerfulness (6:1–18)

From practical behaviour, Jesus turns to specifically religious duties. Giving to the needy, praying and fasting were all appointed by God in the Old Testament as important religious exercises. Running through the teaching at this point is a warning about parading these religious duties before men in order to be commended by those who see us doing them. What matters is this: what does God see?

On *giving to the needy* (vv. 2–4), Jesus commends charity work that is not recorded, reported or even observed! Christ's image is striking—let your right hand give away without even your left hand noticing! The problem is not just that we like being congratulated by others: we also enjoy being congratulated by ourselves. In Christ's kingdom, however, the greatest motive for our deeds of charity ought to be that God will have all the glory in what we do.

Jesus' teaching on *prayer* in verses 5–15 is one of the best-known passages in the Bible because of the model prayer he gives his followers. He warns us in this passage about the danger of religious formalism. When is a prayer not a prayer? When it is a matter of public performance (v. 5), or of empty phrases strung together (v. 7), or when we ask God for something that we are not willing to grant to others (v. 15).

On the other hand, prayer that is genuinely offered to God in the secret place of our lives and that becomes a discipline by which we discover what we need (v. 8)—which often is not the same as what we want—is a gloriously liberating religious exercise. It is prayer to a father, the language of sonship. Jesus is teaching us that we may approach God with the same form of address as belongs to him—the language of a son. Paul makes the same point in Romans 8:15: 'For you did not receive the spirit of slavery to fall back into fear, but you have received the Spirit of adoption as sons, by whom we cry, "Abba! Father!"'

This model prayer is concerned in the first instance with the glory of God. Before we ask anything for ourselves, we look for the hallowing of God's name, the extending of God's kingdom and the doing of God's will. These are the issues that weed out all that is self-centred in our prayer lives. It's not just a matter of coming with our requests: it is coming with requests for things that will give glory to God, that will be in the interests of his gospel and that will produce more obedience to him in our own lives and in the lives of others.

Then we can start asking. We can ask for our needs to be

met in the present, for forgiveness for the past and for protection in the future. By asking God for 'our daily bread', we acknowledge that all our material possessions are his to give and his to withhold. This is the language of dependence on the giver of all good gifts. By asking him to 'forgive us our debts', we are acknowledging a lifetime of accumulating debts we cannot repay before a God who can forgive. And by asking that he 'lead us not into temptation', we are looking forward realistically, knowing that we need to be kept and protected every step of life's way.

It is possible for this model prayer to become a set of 'empty phrases', such as Jesus warns against in verse 7. There is certainly nothing wrong with using this prayer; after all, Jesus teaches us these words. But he also says we are to pray 'like this', that is, to ensure that our prayers reflect this pattern and paradigm. The Westminster Larger Catechism summarizes it well when it says, 'The Lord's prayer is not only for direction, as a pattern, according to which we are to make other prayers; but may also be used as a prayer, so that it be done with understanding, faith, reverence, and other graces necessary to the right performance of the duty of prayer.'[4]

The third religious practice mentioned here is *fasting* (vv. 16–18), abstaining from food for a particular period. As with prayer and deeds of charity, Jesus assumes that his disciples will fast. Again, the main warning is against a mere outward show of religion, fasting with the motive of being seen (and praised) by men.

It is important to note that, although Jesus' teaching appears to be radical, what he is actually doing is recovering the lostheaven message of the Old Testament. It is radical in the real meaning of the word: 'radical' comes from the Latin word *radix*, which means 'root'. In the Old Testament, God required charity, prayer and fasting, but he always insisted that these should be offerings of the heart. The Lord is bringing his disciples back to the true meaning of the Old Testament, as opposed to the meaning imposed on it by the religious teachers and leaders of his day.

Promises of faithfulness (6:19–34)

In the next section of the Sermon, Jesus outlines the blessings that flow from such obedience to him. If we give God the place in our lives that he is due, then we will know his care of us and will be delivered from anxiety and worry.

> If our hearts and our treasures are in heaven, we will have something solid and lasting that can never be removed from us.

In this section, Jesus draws a contrast between earthly possessions and heavenly ones. All that we have here is liable to decay and may even be stolen from us. But if our hearts and our treasures are in heaven, we will have something solid and lasting that can never be removed from us. Jesus warns against a divided heart: it is impossible for both God and possessions to be our masters. The heart can be devoted to one master only.

To be devoted to Jesus Christ is to be freed from the anxiety and worry that so often characterize the fallen world in which we live. Jesus identifies three sources of anxiety: our bodies (we worry over the length of our lives and the state of our health), our food (we worry over what we will eat and drink, over diets and fats and carbohydrates) and our clothes (we worry about being in fashion or out of fashion). Jesus teaches us that 'the Gentiles'—those who have no covenant relationship to God—'seek after all these things' (v. 32).

But in the kingdom of heaven things are different. We have a Father who cares for us; if he gives such attention to the impersonal creation, will he not meet the needs of his own people? If we prioritize 'the kingdom of God and his righteousness' (v. 33), we shall lack nothing.

Principles of holiness (7:1–29)

In all of this, Jesus is building up to the climax of his Sermon: those whom God has blessed, and for whom the heavenly Father provides, are called to be holy. That means, first, being *slow to judge others* (vv. 1–6). We can so easily be critical of others when we have not been critical of ourselves, pointing out minute failings in others while ignoring huge lapses in our own lives. Holiness is sensitive to the world of sin that is in our own hearts and it guards the things of God against misuse, either by ourselves or by others (v. 6).

Second, holiness means *remaining dependent on God* (vv. 7–11). Asking, seeking and knocking are all forms of application—we come to God with requests. Jesus uses a form of argument here in which he begins with what is mundane and rises to what is heavenly—an argument from the lesser thing to the greater. If human beings can grant requests to one another, our heavenly Father will certainly give good things to those who apply to him for them.

Third, holiness means *walking Christ's road* (vv. 12–14). Many people quote the so-called 'golden rule' of verse 12 without considering the choice explicit in verses 13–14. We can only do good to others as we are committed to Christ. That means entering through the narrow gate and walking the narrow way.

Fourth, holiness means *bearing good fruit* (vv. 15–23). In one of the most solemn passages in the Bible, Jesus warns against the possibility of giving every appearance of piety, godliness and spirituality, yet remaining at a distance from God. False prophets are like wolves dressed as sheep. God's people, on the other hand, are to be like healthy trees, bearing good fruit, otherwise there is the danger of coming to Christ at last with the profession of orthodoxy and the badge of supernatural works, only for him to say, 'I never knew you' (v. 23).

Fifth, holiness means *building on the right foundation* (vv. 24–27). The parable of the two builders is well known. One built on the sand, the other on the rock. In Luke's version of the parable, the rock was found by digging deep under the surface (Luke 6:48). So it is what is under the surface that is important; when the test comes, the strength of our foundation is the only thing that matters. The distinction here is not between those who hear Jesus and those who do not, but between those who hear and obey and those who hear but do not obey.

In giving this Sermon, it was evident that Jesus spoke with authority (v. 29)—he was a king with prophetic gifts and a prophet with regal authority.

FOR FURTHER STUDY

1. Compare the call of the disciples in 4:18–22 with the call of Matthew himself in 9:9. What do these passages teach us about entering into discipleship and following Jesus?
2. Can you find traces of Isaiah 61:1–3 in the beatitudes of 5:3–12?
3. Compare 5:14 with John 8:12. What are the similarities and differences between these two verses?
4. In 7:1 we are told not to judge. In 7:6 we are told not to give what is holy to the dogs. How can we keep the requirement of verse 6 without judging who are 'dogs'?
5. Read Luke 6:46–49. How does it compare or contrast with Matthew's account in 7:24–27?

TO THINK ABOUT AND DISCUSS

1. How can our righteousness exceed that of the scribes and Pharisees (5:20)?
2. How would our worship be improved if we applied the principles of 5:23–24?
3. Who are your enemies (see 5:44)? Do you pray for them?
4. Do you use the Lord's Prayer in the normal course of your worship? How can we make proper use of the Lord's Prayer in our devotional lives?
5. In the light of 6:31, do you think that Christians should purchase insurance for the contents of their homes?
6. Is the so-called 'golden rule' of 7:12 a sufficient guide for our lives?

4 The King works miracles

(8:1–9:38)

Jesus demonstrates his uniqueness by his words, but also by his actions. He comes with power into people's lives and transforms them. There is a unique glory to Jesus' approach to people, as a result of which they are never the same again.

The King's works: how does his kingdom advance? (8:1–9:38)

The first miracle performed by Jesus that is recorded in Matthew's Gospel is the healing of the leper (8:1–4), which is followed by the healings of the centurion's servant (8:5–13), Peter's mother-in-law (8:14–15), 'all who were sick' (8:16), two demon-possessed men (8:28–34), a paralysed man (9:1–8), Jairus' daughter and the woman with the discharge (9:18–26), two blind men (9:27–31) and a man who cannot speak (9:32–34). The only non-healing miracle in these chapters is that of Jesus calming the storm (8:23–27).

Why does Matthew emphasize the healing miracles? At one level, he is reminding us that the kingdom of heaven is *not just a matter of words, but also a matter of action.* The Sermon on the Mount is counterbalanced by the activity of Jesus in these miracles. He does not just bring saving words, he also performs saving actions. There is a doctrinal aspect to his work and there is a practical aspect to his work. He teaches profound truths and he changes lives in profound ways. Indeed, his works authenticate his words and demonstrate him to be the Messiah of God (see Acts 10:38).

Yet both Jesus' words and his actions *point to his saving activity.* Matthew's quotation of Isaiah 53:4 in 8:17 is very important. The prophet said that the Messiah would take our illnesses and bear our diseases; in the context of Isaiah 53, the prophet is revealing that dealing with sickness is like dealing with the symptom of a much deeper problem—the problem of our sin. Sin brought sickness into the world. So the Messiah would come in order to deal with the problem at its root and at its heart. Matthew tells us that the miracles of healing are part of Jesus' assault on Satan's kingdom.

The healing miracles also remind us of *the difference Jesus makes in the lives of men and women.* They will never be the same again. Their sick, diseased, demon-possessed relatives are cured, and homes that have been torn apart in physical and emotional distress are now brought to know 'shalom', the peace that comes through wholeness.

Healings (8:1–9:8)

The first of the miracles, the healing of the leper, with its reference to the priests in 8:4, is a reminder to us of the priestly function of the Messiah. In the Old Testament, it was the priest who dealt with skin diseases such as leprosy (see Lev. 13–14). So Jesus fulfils kingly, prophetic and priestly functions. The healing of the leper is an immediate act of Jesus, a response to a passionate plea.

The second miracle, the healing of the centurion's servant (8:5–13), is a reminder to us of Jesus' concern to extend the kingdom beyond the Jewish world. In his encounter with a Roman soldier, we again have the principle of Jesus reaching out that we saw when the wise men came to worship him as a child. All this anticipates the Great Commission to all the nations. What is interesting here is the centurion's great faith (v. 10), which contrasts with the disciples' 'little faith' (v. 26). Those whom we would expect to have great faith only have little faith, while those whom we might expect to have no faith at all show great trust in Jesus. For the centurion, Jesus heals the servant at a distance, rewarding the absolute confidence that the centurion puts in him.

Many come to Jesus because of his healing power. Most of them seek healing for the sick and the demon-possessed (8:16), but others are drawn to volunteer to follow him in discipleship (8:18–22). At first, the paragraph on the cost of following Jesus seems out of place, until we realize what Matthew is telling us—that we cannot follow Christ just for the benefits. The healer has popularity but nowhere to lay his head (8:20). His claim is absolute.

Even those who were his disciples needed to learn the importance of absolute confidence in Jesus. While the centurion trusted the ability of an absent Christ, the disciples could not trust the power of a present Christ. The miracle of the calming of the storm was a means of showing to them the absolute power of Christ over all of nature; but more than this, it was a confirmation to their weak faith of his glory and of the majesty of his kingly person (see John's statement in John 2:11 that when Jesus turned the water into wine, he 'manifested his glory [and] his disciples believed in him').

The healing of the demon-possessed men in 8:28–34 seems simply to be adding another healing miracle to the collection, but here the conflict with Satan is made explicit as the demons say to Jesus, 'What have you to do with us, O Son of God? Have you come here to torment us before the time?' (v. 29). These words reveal that the work of Jesus is essentially a battle between two opposing kingdoms—light and darkness, heaven and hell, and grace and sin are engaged in conflict. The resolution of this particular conflict, in which the demons enter a herd of pigs who subsequently drown, causing the people to banish Jesus from their region, raises some difficulties. What, for example, do pigs have to do with demons? And is Jesus not robbing the herdsmen of their livelihood? We can respond to these by highlighting three effects of this incident. First, it again shows Jesus' concern to bring the gospel into the Gentile world. At another level, it reminds us that the lives of the men are of infinitely greater

The work of Jesus is essentially a battle between two opposing kingdoms—light and darkness, heaven and hell, and grace and sin are engaged in conflict.

value than their possessions. At a further level, it confirms to us the teaching of the Sermon on the Mount on the relative values of life and possessions.

The healing of the paralysed man (9:1–8) brings this section to a climax, as here Jesus demonstrates the relationship between physical and spiritual healing and helps us to understand that healing diseases is never an end in itself but a proof that 'the Son of Man has authority on earth to forgive sins' (9:6). Jesus' claim to forgive sins gives rise to thoughts in the hearts of some that he is blaspheming (9:3), since forgiving sins is a prerogative of God. However, the miracle demonstrates that the lesser power (to heal the sick) is included in the greater (to forgive sins) and that what he is doing anticipates the cross.

Callings (9:9–38)

The description of the call of Matthew (9:9–13) is important because it names the tax collector who would write this Gospel record. The healing miracles have been reported anonymously but now Matthew is named. Some scholars doubt that he is the Levi of Luke 5:27–32, but the content and context of the call narratives are so similar that it is difficult to sustain this position. Matthew's call was quite unexpected, since tax collectors were so despised. They were local people who worked for the Romans and made easy money for themselves in the process. The low view people had of them is seen in the way the religious leaders were amazed that Jesus would eat with tax collectors (9:11), and also in the way Jesus himself spoke of them (in 18:17, for example).

Jesus' explanation, 'I came not to call the righteous, but

sinners' (9:13), is an important interpretative comment on his ministry. The demons recognized that Jesus had 'come' (8:29), but the issue is not about Jesus coming to a specific geographical location; Matthew is referring 'to the advent of Jesus into the world which is in the grip of evil forces'.[1] So when Jesus says that he has come to call sinners, he is reminding us, at one level, of his own pre-existence and, at another level, of his special commission to save those who are far from God.[2]

So far, then, we have seen how the kingdom of heaven advances as Jesus heals the sick, gradually demonstrating the connection between healing and forgiveness, reminding people of the cost of discipleship and calling men personally to follow him, in spite of the prejudices of others.

Jesus' earlier teaching on fasting is supplemented as a result of a question from the disciples of John (9:14–17). Interestingly, Jesus' response is that it is not appropriate for the disciples to fast while he is with them. Fasting is a means of seeking the presence and face of God; in the person of Jesus Christ, God was with his people. The references to new cloth on old clothes and new wine in old wineskins are pointers to the 'newness' of Jesus' teaching, as well as to the 'newness' of the life which he offers.

The miracle stories continue with the reference to the healing of Jairus' daughter (on the basis of the parallel accounts in Mark 5 and Luke 8) and of the woman with the discharge of blood (9:18–26). For twelve years the woman had been afflicted with this condition; for twelve years the ruler of the synagogue had watched his little daughter grow. In the case of the woman, great faith is again commended as she reasons that just to touch the hem of Jesus' cloak will be enough for her (9:22). In the case of the girl, we have the first of three encounters with death, as Jesus calls the girl, who has just slipped into the sleep of death, to wake up. The miracles thus continue to bring us to a climax. The symptoms of sin are seen, not just in sickness and disease, but ultimately in death. Here is one who is able to deal with death.

The miracle of the healing of the blind men (9:27–31) continues to identify Jesus. It is to the 'Son of David' that they call for the restoration of their sight (9:27). This was how Matthew introduced Jesus in 1:1. It is the royal Son who is advancing on the kingdom of darkness, again commending the faith of those who call to him to help. Jesus bids them remain quiet, but his reputation spreads.

Finally, the restoration of speech to the mute man (9:32–34) is testimony to the glory and uniqueness of this great work of Jesus. Nothing has been done like it before in Israel (9:33), not even in the greatest moments of Israel's history. The hatred and spite of the Pharisees breathes through the accusation that Jesus himself must have a demon to deal with demons as he does. The argument is flawed but the hostility is real. The kingdom of darkness against which Jesus is advancing has its advocates and representatives in high places. Perhaps the Roman Empire is not the biggest threat after all.

The passage ends with a statement about the need for labourers to go into the harvest (9:37–38). The more Jesus travelled, and the more he healed, the more his heart was opened in compassion to the harassed crowds. The theme of help for lost people, through apostles commissioned to go out with the gospel, acts as a bridge to the next teaching section of this Gospel.

FOR FURTHER STUDY

1. Like that of Jesus, Moses' ministry was marked by powerful signs and wonders. How does Deuteronomy 34:10–12 use this fact? What were these signs and wonders? How do the miracles of Moses compare with the miracles of Jesus?
2. Look again at the contrast between the faith of the centurion in 8:10 and that of the disciples in 8:26. Why should this have been the case?
3. When Jesus called Matthew to follow him, Matthew was a tax collector. How does Jesus highlight the position of tax collectors in 18:17? Which tax collector found salvation in Luke 19?
4. How does Daniel 7:13 use the phrase 'son of man'? What is the connection between the Son of Man healing and the Son of Man forgiving sins, according to 9:6? Can you find other instances where the title 'Son of Man' is used of Jesus in the Gospels? Who calls him the Son of Man?
5. Jesus raised the daughter of Jairus from death. Whom did he raise from the dead in Luke 7:11–17? And in John 11:43–44? How do these miracles prepare the way for the resurrection?

TO THINK ABOUT AND DISCUSS

1. What do you think was the purpose of the healing miracles in Jesus' ministry and in the ministry of the early church?
2. Do you think that such miracles continue in the church today? In the light of the New Testament, why might some people argue that miracles do continue? Why might others argue that they have ceased with the close of the New Testament Scripture?
3. How important is the concept of 'calling' in the life of discipleship? Would you distinguish a call to discipleship in general from a call to specific types of Christian service (for example, missions or ministry)?

5 The King calls followers

(10:1–12:50)

Jesus sends his people into a hostile world to serve him and live for him there. He has standards which he expects his people to follow, and encouragements which he gives to them.

The King's followers: what is it like to serve him? (10:1–11:30)

The second major teaching block of Matthew's Gospel begins in chapter 10 and concerns the mission on which Jesus is sending his apostles. But it should not be taken in isolation from the wider context, which seems to have as its theme the service of the Lord of the kingdom. Not only do we find him speaking to the apostles, we also find him giving encouragement to John the Baptist, speaking out against the cities that refused to serve him and demonstrating that he, Lord of all, is the Servant of Jehovah.

Commissioning those who will serve (10:1–42)

This section begins with the names of the twelve disciples to whom Jesus delegates authority to assault Satan's kingdom as he is doing (10:1–4). These are thc ones Jesus 'sent out' (v. 5), which in the original Greek is the verb that gives us the word 'apostle'.

The list of names begins with Simon Peter, who is always given a place of pre-eminence in the listing of the apostles, not just because of what Jesus will say to him in 16:18, but also because of the foundational and important role Peter will play in the story of the early church. There are two sets of brothers listed. Matthew identifies himself by his previous employment as tax collector and Judas is identified as the one who betrayed Jesus. These apostles were the first gifts of Jesus to the New Testament church (Eph. 4:11). They were ordinary people through whom Jesus would do extraordinary things.

Four things stand out in this commissioning passage:

The work Jesus gives his people to do (vv. 5–15)

The *place* of their work is to be among 'the lost sheep of the house of Israel' (v. 6). We have already seen that Matthew is preparing the way for the universal proclamation of the gospel—wise men from the east have already worshipped Jesus and a Roman soldier has been commended for his faith. One day, disciples will be made in all the nations (28:19). But Jesus is reflecting the unique purpose of God in the mission to the world—Israel is the light of all the nations (see Isa. 42:6; 49:6; 60:3). God 'had chosen Israel in relation to his purpose for the world, not just for Israel'.[1] Yet there was still much that had to be accomplished in Israel up until the death, resurrection and ascension of Jesus. Only after Pentecost would the Christian mission extend among the Gentiles and the Samaritans.

The *content* of their work is to continue proclaiming the message that Jesus himself has preached: 'The kingdom of heaven is at hand' (v. 7). Like his teaching, theirs is to be accompanied and authenticated by miracles of healing, resurrection and exorcism.

The *provision* for their work is to be met entirely by God himself. They are to take no gold or silver, no excess baggage, no staff. God will make provision for them through the hospitality of those who will receive their message. The apostles are to approach all communities in peaceable ways and for peaceful purposes. If they are not received, they are to withdraw. God will deal with the hard-hearted cities who refuse to come to him, just as he will make provision for those who serve him.

The cost of obedience to Jesus (vv. 16–25)

Jesus dismisses any romantic notion of what it means to be his servant. His people may be like sheep, but they are like sheep among wolves (v. 16), constantly harassed and endangered. For that reason, they need to be aware of several things.

First, their approach to others needs to be a combination of wisdom and innocence. Jesus wishes his servants to be 'wise as serpents', to be cunning and pragmatic, yet combining it with the innocence of 'doves'.

Second, they are to be realistic with regard to the way in which others will treat them. Matthew writes from within the church community which has suffered the indignities that Jesus predicted: being made answerable to governors, kings and Gentiles. Courts and synagogues will afford no refuge; indeed, they may be the places of greatest threat and danger (v. 17). So, too, may families; siblings will have no compunction about betraying their Christian brothers or sisters, and it is not beyond the bounds of possibility that parents and children may betray one another (v. 21). Indeed, Jesus enlarges it to predict that 'you will be hated by all for my name's sake' (v. 22). If Jesus has suffered the indignity of being named 'Beelzebul' (v. 25), his followers should not expect exemption from such trials.

Third, in the midst of such trials, Christ's apostles are to be free from anxiety. Trials and persecutions will come, but the apostles will not be left without help. On the one hand, the Holy Spirit will help them; on the other, they are to remember that they are walking in Christ's footsteps (vv. 24–25). There is an important and interesting Trinitarian perspective to these encouragements: the Spirit who will speak through God's people is the 'Spirit of your Father' (v. 20), and the hatred will be 'for my name's sake', according to Jesus (v. 22). This anticipates the Great Commission, which promises the enduring presence of Jesus through the Spirit.

Fourth, the apostles are to work and witness with the end always in view (v. 22). It is the one who endures to the end who will be saved (the same phrase appears in 24:13). What is that end? Matthew says that it is the coming of the Son of Man (v. 23). This anticipates the teaching of later chapters, in which the appearance of the Son of Man is shown to be the point to which all of history is moving. The apostles are to face a lifetime of costly witness always keeping their eyes on the goal of the coming of the Son of Man and praying for persevering, enduring grace.

The encouragement they have in their service (vv. 26–33)

Once again, Jesus says to the apostles that they ought not to be afraid (v. 26). There are several reasons for being free from anxiety.

First, God's servants will be publicly vindicated. Here they may be subjected to much persecution, as plans against them forged in secret and under the cover of darkness are translated into action. Such plans can go far; Christ's apostles may be killed as a result. However, their souls are immortal, and Jesus encourages them to remember that God will bring everything at last to the light of his judgement and his justice, and that there is no ultimate danger for his people.

Second, God's servants are highly valued. Sparrows are valuable (v. 29; compare 6:26). They are valuable to people, but supremely they are valuable to God. If God looks after his creatures to the extent that not one of them can fall to the ground unnoticed, how much more will he look after his servants? He knows even the number of hairs on the heads of his servants.

Third, God's servants will be openly acknowledged. The apostles are being sent to testify to the greatness of Jesus. Their work in the world is to confess him. But Jesus' promise is that before his Father he will confess his people (v. 32).

The explanation as to why it must be like this (vv. 34–42)

In all of this, Christ's servants are to bear in mind the nature of his mission. In stark terms, he describes his mission as bringing a 'sword' to the earth (v. 34). It will be a sword of division, in which the closest blood ties will be severed in the interests of spiritual ties of loyalty to Jesus Christ. Indeed, he demands total and primary loyalty, promising that to submit completely and wholly to him is, in fact, to 'find' one's life (v. 39).

The close connection between the work of Jesus and that of his apostles is also part of the explanation. Jesus tells the apostles that 'Whoever receives you receives me' (v. 40). Jesus will not overlook deeds of kindness towards his apostles; they will be regarded as if carried out towards himself.

Encouraging those who have served (11:1–19)

Matthew carefully turns our attention from the apostles, on the brink of their service, to John the Baptist, who is coming to the end of his. He has been imprisoned and sends his disciples to Jesus to ask if he is the one who was to come (v. 3). At one level, it is a surprising question from someone whose whole ministry was designed to demonstrate that Jesus was indeed the one who would do remarkable things among men (see 3:11–12). For this reason, some have suggested that John's purpose was to encourage the disciples whom he personally sent to Jesus.

However, Jesus' answer is directed to John; and this is the clue to help us realize that John is facing serious doubt and uncertainty. He has seen the miracles, but something does not fit his understanding of the messianic prophecies. After all, John has preached that Jesus would baptize with fire, would thresh with a winnowing fork and would burn the chaff (3:12). To date, there has been no obvious act of judgement.

Jesus sends the disciples back with an answer that draws heavily on Isaiah 61:1. There the Messiah was predicted as one anointed to bring good news to the poor, to bind up the broken-hearted, to proclaim liberty to the captives and to open the prisons to the bound. Jesus is telling John that the messianic purpose has begun to be realized among men. While John is looking for more evidence of this, Jesus asks him to be content with the evidence there is and not count it for too little.

The gospel is being preached and is authenticated by the miracles of healing and of resurrection. Isaiah went further and spoke of Messiah judging the nations; Jesus does not refer to this. This will take place in God's time. John has to be content with the inauguration of Christ's kingdom, and not be offended.

The whole episode gives Jesus opportunity to explain the significance of the ministry of John. The reason for this may be in part to restore John's reputation following the message from prison; however, Jesus' main function is to show how the very messianic purpose intimated in the Old Testament included the ministry of John. The citation of Malachi 3:1 in 11:10 demonstrates that John is the 'messenger' who was to herald the coming of Jesus, and the 'Elijah' who was predicted in Malachi 4:5.

Jesus describes John as the greatest man ever born (v. 11); yet, comparatively speaking, the 'least' of those now in the kingdom of Christ is greater than John. Jesus' words are an indication of the superiority of the new administration of God's plan of salvation which has been inaugurated in his coming and in his teaching.

The reception that John received is also mirrored in the reception that Jesus himself has received. People are fickle; disappointed expectations lead to simplistic explanations. John's lifestyle led to his being called a devil (v. 18); Jesus' friendship with sinners became an occasion of accusation and mockery (v. 19). Yet the service of John has been highly valued by God.

Denouncing those who will not serve (11:20–24)

In contrast with the willing service of John, which has led to his imprisonment, is the unwillingness of many to serve Jesus Christ. There is a deep contrast in this passage between cities like Chorazin and Bethsaida, which saw the mighty works of Jesus, and cities like Tyre and Sodom, which did not. Although all the inhabitants of these cities will face the judgement of God, God's assessment of their rebellion and lack of repentance will be just and will consider the privileges involved. In a nuclear war or accident, the damage depends on the level of radiation to which people are exposed; in the judgement of God, the damnation depends on the level of privilege and revelation to which people are exposed. The greater our knowledge of gospel truth, the more serious our lack of submission to Christ becomes.

Inviting others to come and serve (11:25–30)

It is interesting that, precisely at the point where Jesus is reflecting on those who have rebelled against his ministry, he says, 'Thank you, Father.' We are (rightly) thankful when people do believe; Jesus is thankful even when they remain stubborn and rebellious. The source of his thankfulness is the fact that God is sovereignly in control of all these matters.

This passage is profoundly important for our understanding of the effectiveness of the gospel, as well as for our approach to gospel evangelism. On the one hand, Jesus emphasizes the absolute sovereignty of God in the matter of salvation. No one can be saved apart from God revealing himself to sinners. And God reveals himself only to those sinners whom he chooses. It may be a difficult doctrine but it is unmistakeably part of the gospel of Jesus: 'no one knows the Father except the Son and anyone to whom the Son chooses to reveal him' (v. 27). Jesus' choice of us precedes our choice of him.

On the one hand, Jesus emphasizes the absolute sovereignty of God in the matter of salvation. No one can be saved apart from God revealing himself to sinners ... Yet no one is saved without choosing Christ.

Yet no one is saved without choosing Christ. That is why, on the other hand, the doctrine of God's sovereignty in salvation is to be taken hand in hand with the full and free offer of the gospel, written so majestically in these words: 'Come to me' (v. 28). Jesus offers himself and promises rest. He promises freedom from sin's burden under his own yoke. His call is not to the strong and self-sufficient, but to the weak and the weary. These are the twin themes of all our gospel work: the sovereignty of God and the responsibility of man. These are not equally final: we must always give the priority in the work of the gospel to God's absolute sovereignty. But we must do so in a way that also does justice to the responsibility of each one of us to respond to the voice of the King.

The King who comes to serve (12:1–50)

Matthew 12 weaves together a remarkable tapestry of pictures and images of Jesus. Let's think about them. Who is Jesus? He is ...

Lord of the Sabbath (vv. 1–14)

Jesus was involved in controversy over Sabbath-keeping for virtually his entire ministry. In this section, his disciples are criticized for plucking grains of corn and eating them on the Sabbath day. Jesus defends the disciples against the charge of Sabbath-breaking by referring to 1 Samuel 21, where David ate the bread put aside for the priests. Although the bread was dedicated to God and therefore 'holy', God was not going to condemn David for eating it. The purity of the temple was not compromised by the king's action. Now something greater than the temple (v. 6) has come in the person of Jesus, who is 'lord of the Sabbath'.

If the primitive Christian confession was that 'Jesus is Lord' (see 1 Cor. 12:3), then that includes his lordship over the Sabbath. He was not Lord of the Sabbath only for the duration of his three years of public ministry; he remains Lord of the Sabbath now. The Sabbath, as a creation ordinance, is of perpetual significance; and in Christ we have the incarnate King, the God of the Old Testament who gave Sinai's law to his people and the Sabbath rest to man, now among us, exercising the authority that is his alone.

That Lordship is seen in the miracle by which Jesus heals a man and shows that mercy is more acceptable to God than mere legalism (vv. 9–14).

Servant of Jehovah (vv. 15–21)

Yet, at the same time, the King is Servant! By citing Isaiah 42:1–3 in this section of his Gospel, Matthew reminds us that Jesus has come to serve. The quotation also explains Jesus' reluctance to publicize who he is and what he is doing (v. 16). The time for that would come. At present, the Servant, as Isaiah predicted, will not 'cry aloud'; nor will anyone 'hear his voice in the streets'. Nonetheless, he who is Lord is among men in the form of a servant, equipped by the Spirit to do the Father's will and sent to proclaim good news to the Gentiles.

Son of Man (vv. 22–37)

The vexed question about blasphemy against the Holy Spirit actually focuses more on the identity of Jesus than on the Spirit himself. In the context, some of the religious leaders have accused Jesus of casting out demons by a demonic power. Jesus' response is perfectly logical: why would someone possessed by Satan want to drive Satan out of someone else's life? To ascribe the power of Jesus to Satan when in actual fact his empowering is the direct result of the Spirit's ministry (Acts 10:38) is to blaspheme the name of God. To remain opposed to the Spirit's testimony to the identity of Jesus is a sin for which no forgiveness can be found.

This means that we must weigh our words carefully. Words of blasphemy bring forth Jesus' wrath. Our words, according to Jesus, show the condition of our hearts (v. 34). That is why Jesus can say that words will either condemn us or justify us (v. 37), since they reveal our true character. Of course, the words of Jesus are subject to the same principle and they reveal his own condition and his own heart.

Greater than Jonah (vv. 38–41)

The prophet Jonah was commissioned by God to preach in Nineveh but instead ran away from his responsibility. God brought him back to his duty through a process of humbling and repentance, which included spending three days and three nights inside a great fish (Jonah 1:17). Jesus here underscores the fact that the Book of Jonah is not legend or fable but historical fact; more than that, he sees it as a prefiguring of his own descent into death for the same period.

Jesus' purpose in alluding to Jonah, however, is not so much to make this comparison as to demonstrate the different responses between the people of Nineveh, who heard Jonah preach and repented of their sins, and the people of Jesus' generation, who have heard a 'greater than

Jonah' and have not repented. Again, the seriousness of the rejection is seen in the light of the greatness of the privilege.

Greater than Solomon (vv. 42–45)

The same point is made in the comparison with Solomon. Jesus refers to the visit of the queen of Sheba (1 Kings 10:1), who travelled a great distance to hear Solomon's wisdom. The people of Galilee and its environs have Jesus, David's greater Son, preaching the gospel, yet they show little interest. The reference to an unclean spirit returning to the life from which it has been banished, as a result of which that life is worse than ever, seems to tie in with this emphasis on the consequences of rejecting Jesus.

Elder brother and co-worker (vv. 46–50)

The theme of service is taken up at the close of the chapter. It seems somewhat harsh for Jesus to respond to the news that his family are at the door with the question: 'Who is my mother, and who are my brothers?' Yet his emphasis is on the spiritual family of God in the world, characterized, as he is himself, by doing the will of God.

In all of these ways we see different perspectives of the King who has come to serve and who calls others into his kingdom to serve God, too.

FOR FURTHER STUDY

1. Read the following passages: Acts 1:21–26; 1 Corinthians 12:27–31; Ephesians 4:7–12. What do they teach about the unique role of the apostles?
2. Jesus highlights the importance of 'enduring to the end' (10:22). Look at James 5:7–11 and Revelation 2:10. What do these passages say about this topic? Are they contradicted by Hebrews 6:4–6?
3. What does James say about Elijah in James 5:17? Given the comparison between John and Elijah in Matthew 11:14, what should we learn for ourselves from John's questions and doubts?
4. Jesus declared himself to be Lord of the Sabbath (12:8). How do the following passages enable us to understand this: Mark 2:27–28; John 5:16–17; John 9:14–17; John 20:19; Revelation 1:10?
5. Matthew cites the prophecy of Isaiah, in which the Messiah is called a servant (Matt. 12:18, citing Isa. 42:1). How do the following passages help us to understand Jesus as Servant: Matthew 26:39; John 6:38; Philippians 2:5–8; Hebrews 5:8; 1 Peter 2:18–21?
6. How does the Book of Jonah help us to understand Jesus better (see Matt. 12:40)?

TO THINK ABOUT AND DISCUSS

1. Is it reasonable for Jesus to demand that we love him more than our parents? How does this relate to the fifth commandment (Exod. 20:12)? What does it tell us about the nature of discipleship and family life?
2. In the light of 11:22, can we talk about various degrees of punishment in eternity? What about varying degrees of blessing?
3. In our presentation of the gospel, should we try to explain that God's sovereignty does not contradict our responsibility?
4. What do you understand by 'blasphemy against the Spirit' (12:31)?
5. Can we belong to the family of Jesus (12:50)?

6 The King tells stories

(13:1–58)

Matthew's story includes Jesus' stories. Many readers of the New Testament are familiar with Jesus' parables, but their significance goes deeper than mere story-telling. They function in order both to explain and to conceal his kingdom. In this third teaching block of his gospel, Matthew brings several parables together that shed light on how the kingdom operates.

Purpose of the parables (vv. 10–17,34–35,51–2)

The parables of Jesus have been described as 'earthly stories with heavenly meanings'. While there is an element of truth in that description, it does not do justice to the purpose of these parables that Matthew has gathered together in chapter 13. In his Gospel, these parables are set immediately after the account of widespread hostility to Jesus and rejection of his message, and they serve to explain to us why that hostility exists.

The parables are not simply illustrations of Jesus' teaching, in the way a preacher might tell a story to illuminate a point. They are key elements of his teaching and focus our attention in a special way onto the theme of the kingdom. Scattered throughout chapter 13 are three reasons for the parables.

First, by speaking in parables, Jesus fulfilled prophecy. The psalmist had declared himself to be a speaker of parables (Ps. 78:2, cited in 13:35). Matthew sees this as prophetic; it is no surprise to us to find Jesus speaking in parables because that was what the Messiah would do.

Second, by speaking in parables, Jesus caused division. In answer to the disciples' question 'Why do you speak to them in parables?' Jesus answers, 'To you it has been given to know the secrets of the kingdom of heaven, but to them it has not been given' (13:10–11). The double emphasis on what has been 'given' is an echo and reflection of the sovereignty of God in the matter of salvation. Jesus is pointing out that there are elements to do with the kingdom of heaven which are mysterious. Part of that mystery is that, as the gospel is proclaimed by Jesus, some believe and some do not; and the effect is that, at this present time, faith and unbelief exist side by side.

The citation of Isaiah 6:9–10 in 13:14–15 is a reminder to us that God can send his word with a purpose of judgement as well as of salvation. The sun which melts the wax hardens the clay; and the word which opens the hearts of some to receive Christ confirms others in their rebellion, rejection and unbelief. The parables become doors by which some enter into the glories of the kingdom, while others are shut out from its blessings. If we understand the parables, it is a sign that we are shut in. If we don't, it is a sign that we are shut out. One thing is certain: when Jesus speaks, and when the gospel is preached, there is always a response.

Third, by speaking in parables, Jesus confirmed faith. At the close of the chapter, Jesus asks, 'Have you understood?' (v. 51), echoing their earlier question, 'Why speak like this?' To their affirmative answer, Jesus responds that his concern is solely with the work of the kingdom of God, and that in his teaching his followers will find 'what is new and what is old': new levels of understanding, and confirmation of what they have already learned.

Who is the 'scribe … trained for the kingdom' (v. 52)? It is anyone who understands the teachings of Jesus and can pass them on to others. Matthew himself fits into that category: his Gospel is an example of someone gathering together old things and new things about Jesus, weaving the history of redemption and the life of Jesus of Nazareth together. But what Matthew is doing is what we must all do: not in the sense of writing inspired Scripture, but in teaching and instructing others who would be disciples themselves (28:20).

The sower: parable and explanation (vv. 1–9,18–23)

One of the best-known of Jesus' parables is the parable of the sower. Drawing from a familiar sight—a man sowing seed in a field—Jesus teaches us something about how his kingdom impacts human lives; or, to put it another way, he shows how people actually do enter into his kingdom through their individual experiences of his blessing and power.

Perhaps the story would be better described as the parable of the soils because, as the sower casts the seed out of his hand, it falls onto four different kinds of soil, each giving a different result. We can summarize the parable this way:

Type of soil	Result of contact with seed	Spiritual meaning
The path	Birds swooped down—seed taken away immediately	Hear word, but don't understand it—devil steals it away
Rocky ground	No depth of earth—instant growth but no root, therefore scorched by the sun	Initial reception of gospel message, but persecution leads to falling away
Weeds	Seed grew among thorns that choked it	Reception of word compromised by riches and worldly concerns
Tilled ground	Seed took root and there was growth	Word heard, understood and received—spiritual fruit in human life

There are several layers of meaning and application here. Jesus is reminding us that not all our gospel labour has a positive effect. Sometimes, only a quarter of the labour and effort we exert will be effective in yielding a harvest to God's glory. Like Jesus, we do not give up because of the apparent fruitlessness of our efforts. Matthew 12, as we noted, cites Isaiah 42:1–3; had Matthew wished, he could also have quoted Isaiah 42:4, which explicitly says that the Messiah will not be discouraged.

Jesus is also telling us that the effectiveness of our gospel witness might not be immediately apparent. At the end of a hard day's sowing, the sower had very little to show for his labour. It is not the parable of the 'show-er'! The faithful gospel preacher, like Jesus himself, does not place his confidence on signs of immediate success but in the promise that seedtime and harvest will never fail (see Gen. 8:22). The sower sows in faith, believing that what he does will have a consequence in the future, if not in the immediate present.

Jesus is also telling us that opposition is to be expected, and that there are different ways in which the gospel of the kingdom can be rendered ineffective. Some hear it and reject it immediately. Others hear it and receive it with great emotion; but when they are tested by persecution they fall away. Others embrace it but are soon distracted both by legitimate cares and by illicit pleasures. The kingdom may have appeared in the person of the King, but we can be sure that many will fail to yield to the King's authority.

Weeds: parable and explanation (vv. 24–30,36–43)

Jesus tells another story about sowing. In the first, only a small percentage of the seed fell onto good ground. In this parable, even the good seed is compromised. As the result of a covert operation by an 'enemy' of the sower, the field is sown with weeds among the wheat. To the suggestion that the servants go into the field to take out the weeds, the master says, 'No; you could root up the good growth with the bad. We will separate them at harvest time.'

As with the parable of the sower, Jesus provides an explanation of the meaning. He makes the following point-by-point comparison:

Element of story	Spiritual meaning
Sower	Son of Man (i.e. Jesus himself)
Field	The world
Good seed	Children of the kingdom
Weeds	Children of the evil one
Enemy	Devil
Harvest	End of the world
Reapers	The angels

The comparisons are skilful and simple, and the message is that, in the experience of the kingdom of God in the world, the children of God and the children of the devil co-exist, without separation, until the end of the world comes. Then the angels will gather in the harvest and separate those who belong to Christ from those who belong to the devil.

Although the kingdom has come, the full expression of its reality will be seen at the consummation of history. Then the children of God (the 'righteous') will shine like the sun 'in the kingdom of their Father' (13:43). The kingdom is both present, where two seeds can only be *distinguished* from one another, and future, when they will be *separated*.

Mustard seed and leaven (vv. 31–33)

Once again, Jesus uses the illustration of sowing seeds in a field to teach something about his kingdom. But whereas the parable of the sower might suggest that much sowing is fruitless, the parable of the mustard seed shows how powerful and successful good sowing can be—its effect can be out of all proportion to its appearance. The mustard seed may be the smallest of all seeds, and the yeast may be almost indiscernible in the baking mixture, but the effects produced in both cases are far-reaching and thorough.

Jesus is reminding us that some people (like Matthew himself, perhaps?) find salvation in Jesus Christ when they are not looking for him; others make the same discovery through their careful use of the means appointed for that purpose.

Hidden treasure and a valuable pearl (vv. 44–46)

The Sermon on the Mount spoke about having treasure in heaven; these two parables also use the idea of treasure and value to illustrate what it means to belong to Jesus' kingdom.

The two parables seem to be teaching the same thing—that the kingdom of heaven is like the discovery of something wonderful. But there are subtle differences between the two stories. In the first, the man seems to stumble across the treasure in the field, while, in the second, the discovery is no accident—it is the result of a careful search. Jesus is reminding us that some people (like Matthew himself, perhaps?) find salvation in Jesus Christ when they are not looking for him; others make the same discovery through their careful use of the means appointed for that purpose.

In all cases, however, the discovery is so wonderful that its value eclipses the value of everything else. Nothing can be compared with having, and possessing, the spiritual blessings of the kingdom of God.

The fishing net (vv. 47–50)

Here is another aspect of the way in which the kingdom of heaven works among men and women. Jesus compares the work of the gospel to the way in which men would use a net to catch fish, hurling the net into the sea, then drawing in the catch, prior to separating the good fish from the bad. As with the story of the weeds, therefore, there is an emphasis on the mixture of good and bad drawn in by the workmen of the kingdom, and on the final act of distinguishing between what is valuable and what is not.

This is one of only a few references to fishing in the Gospel of Matthew, but the fact that Peter and Andrew were mending their nets when Jesus called them (4:18–22) shows how relevant the metaphor of the parable was. To use the kind of net Jesus describes here would require co-operation between the fishermen, and to separate the fish that could be eaten or sold from those that would have to be discarded was a vital part of the process.

Applying this to the kingdom, Jesus says that the work of separating people who are 'evil' from those who are 'righteous' will belong to the angels (v. 49; compare v. 39, where the reapers represent the angels). At the end of human history, the angels will accompany those who are saved, who are genuinely righteous, into heaven, and those who are not will be cast into the 'fiery furnace' (v. 50). This final separation is a theme that runs through this Gospel, from the distinction between the two ways in 7:13–14 to the final judgement of chapter 25.

Still rejected (vv. 53–58)

The theme of rejection continues as the teaching block ends and the narrative resumes. Matthew brings us to Jesus' home town of Nazareth, where he continues teaching in the synagogue. Obviously, Matthew is not giving a complete biography of Jesus, since there is much detail about Jesus' experience in his native town that is omitted. That makes his point all the clearer: Jesus' teaching is unique, authoritative and quite unlike anything anyone has heard elsewhere. His lack of formal theological education only deepens the mystery for those who hear Jesus teach.

Jesus' response is to recognize the particular dishonour a prophet receives in his native land. Often it is among one's own people that a minister finds the greatest rejection. It was certainly the case for Jesus, whose work was curtailed because of the unbelief of the people (v. 58).

FOR FURTHER STUDY

1. The parable of the sower and the seed is well known. How are the following passages related to this theme: Isaiah 55:10; 2 Corinthians 9:10; Galatians 6:7?
2. How is the end of the world like gathering in a harvest (Matt. 13:39)?
3. What are the points of comparison and contrast between the parable of the hidden treasure (13:44) and the parable of the pearl (13:45–46)?

TO THINK ABOUT AND DISCUSS

1. Is it right to describe the parables as 'earthly stories with heavenly meanings'?
2. Are the parables illustrations? Explain your answer.
3. How do the parables conceal the kingdom (13:11–17)?
4. In what sense might it still be true that a prophet has honour except in his own house (13:57)?

7 The King meets people

(14:1–16:20)

Jesus' actions and interactions are fascinating. He meets a wide variety of people, some of whom are attracted to him, while others are not. Matthew is honest in his description and he invites us to put ourselves face to face with the King. In this section of the Gospel, therefore, we have an account of some of these meetings as Matthew continues to explore the influence of Jesus on others.

The King and the king (14:1–12)

The story of the death of John the Baptist serves a twofold purpose. First, it closes the important chapter of the Bible on the man whom God sent ahead of Jesus to blaze the trail for him and prepare the people for the coming King. Matthew told us about him in chapter 3; now the forerunner of the heavenly King is beheaded by an earthly king.

Second, it serves to highlight what Herod thinks of Jesus. This is important, because Matthew is going to demonstrate how hostility to Jesus has been growing, with the result that at every level of society there is rejection of him.

The king in question is Herod Antipas, also described as 'Herod the tetrarch'. He was the son of Herod the Great, king at the time of Jesus' birth. He will meet Jesus later during his trial (Luke 23:6–16), as a result of which he will be reconciled to Pilate.

When Herod hears about the growing fame of Jesus and his miracles, his conscience pricks him and all he can think is that John the Baptist must have come back from the dead. He has good reason to think in this way: Herod had divorced his first wife so that he could marry Herodias, the wife of his half-brother, Herod Philip. John denounced the immorality of this action, with the result that Herod threw John into prison. When the daughter of Herodias danced before the king, he promised her anything she asked. It was a rash promise, for she asked for John's head. The price was greater for Herod than it was for John. John died with a clear conscience, but Herod now lives with a guilty one. The reputation of Jesus makes him think that John has come back to haunt him.

The unique ministry of John that had begun in the desert ended in a prison. The disciples of John bury his body and report the matter to Jesus. John had said that he must decrease for Jesus to increase (John 3:30); his decrease was to the point of death. While we call Stephen the first Christian martyr, John became the first New Testament martyr for the cause of truth and righteousness.

The King and the crowd (14:13–21)

Jesus' attempt to steal away for privacy and solitude does not work. Large crowds of people walk to him, hoping for a blessing from him. Matthew tells us that when Jesus saw the crowd 'he had compassion on them'. This is an important indicator of the spirit that motivated Jesus to help needy men and women. B. B. Warfield points out that compassion 'is the emotion which is most frequently attributed to him'.[1] It conveys his reaction to the needs of people. 'The sight of their desperate plight awakens our Lord's pity and moves him to provide the remedy.'[2] Whatever people thought of him, he always thought to do people good.

The practical need to cater for such a large crowd is not lost on the disciples. As they see the evening approaching, they urge Jesus to dismiss the crowd (v. 15). They have no resources with which to feed them. All the food available to them is five loaves and two fish. That is not enough.

Or is it? Jesus takes the food and asks God to bless it. He begins distributing it to the disciples, who in turn give it to the crowd. The food keeps coming as Jesus miraculously multiplies the portion. The result is that 'they all ate and were satisfied' (v. 20). Twelve baskets full of broken pieces are left over. Although we often refer to this as the feeding of the five thousand, Matthew tells us that five thousand is only the number of the men present (v. 21).

Why twelve baskets? One commentator suggests that

'each disciple had a basket of food left for himself, out of which he could share with Jesus'.[3] It does seem as though the number of baskets relates to the number of disciples whom he would send out with the gospel.

The fact that there is so much left over is also a remarkable illustration of the point Jesus made in the Sermon on the Mount, when he encouraged the disciples to trust him for their needs. He told them to pray for daily bread (6:11) and explicitly said to them that they should not be anxious about what to eat or drink (6:31). This miracle is as much for their benefit as for the benefit of the people.

The King and the disciples (14:22–36)

Following the miracle, Jesus has other lessons to teach his disciples. The crowd is dismissed; the disciples are despatched across the sea. Jesus himself goes up a mountain to pray. Mountains are important to Matthew (see 5:1; 28:16). So too is prayer (see 6:1–15; 26:41). Jesus prays to the Father, constantly drawing on his Father's promises to him and seeking his Father's will. In doing so, he gives his people a great example to follow.

While Jesus is alone praying on the mountain, the disciples are experiencing rough weather in the middle of the sea. Suddenly Jesus appears, walking on the water. The disciples are full of fear, an emotion they often experience (see, for example, 17:6). Jesus speaks to them and assures them that it is, in fact, himself.

We are meant, I think, to see a connection between Jesus' prayer and Jesus' presence. Although he was not physically in the boat, he was spiritually present with his disciples.

Their fear was unfounded. Jesus was, in fact, thinking of them, and knew the danger they were in.

Peter's response is to request the ability to walk on the water towards Jesus. He climbs out of the boat onto the surface of the sea and is able to walk slowly towards Jesus. But the sound of the wind distracts him and he begins to sink. His prayer, 'Lord, save me' (v. 30), is immediately answered. Once again, however, the disciples are rebuked for having little faith (see 6:30; 8:26).

The result is that the disciples worship Jesus, acknowledging him to be the Son of God (v. 33). Thus, while several refuse to obey Jesus, there are those who are willing to give him the glory that is his as Lord of the universe, Master of the waves—Jesus, the Son of God. The fame of Jesus continues to spread, and he continues to display his compassion and healing power.

The King and the religious leaders (15:1–9)

The Pharisees and scribes, the Jewish religious leaders, continue to try to trap Jesus in his doctrine and theology. Their accusation on this occasion is that the disciples of Jesus are not honouring the traditions of the elders. The example they choose to illustrate this claim is that the disciples do not wash their hands before eating.

However, as Jesus' response makes clear, the issue is not whether hands are clean or not; the real issue is that tradition, the views and commandments of men, is being substituted for the commandments of God. In the name of religion, personal views are being substituted for the authoritative Word of God.

The quotation given in verses 8–9 from Isaiah 29:13 was fulfilled in these religious leaders: here were people who spoke of God yet failed to honour him, and who elevated the views of sinful men to too high a standard. The result was that they nullified and made void the Word of God.

Behind Jesus' dismissal of the views of the Pharisees is the principle he has been teaching from the outset: that it is the heart that is important to God. The righteousness of the followers of the King must exceed the righteousness of the Pharisees. They are examples of wolves in sheep's clothing (7:15), those who give the appearance of zeal for God but who have no love in their hearts towards him.

The King and the people (15:10–20)

This is the principle that Jesus continues to press home in his teaching of the people. If religion is a matter of externals, it achieves nothing. But if it is genuine, and from the heart, it pleases God. The Pharisees are clearly offended by Jesus' rebuke (v. 12), and this concerns his own disciples. But Jesus does not mince his words. The Pharisees are blind leaders of blind people. Their religion is external. To them, washing hands is important. But to God, a clean heart is important; this was what Jesus stated as one of the first rules of his kingdom (5:8).

The King and the Canaanite woman (15:21–28)

While the disciples are rebuked for their small faith, a Gentile woman is about to be commended for her great faith (v. 28). She comes to Jesus as a result of the spiritual condition of her daughter, crying to him with words that bring together several of the themes of this Gospel: 'Have mercy on me, O Lord, Son of David' (v. 22).

Jesus appears to treat her very harshly. First, he says nothing. As a result of her constant begging of him to help, the disciples become frustrated and agitated, and want her sent away.

Then, he speaks to the disciples, deliberately ignoring the woman. 'I was sent', Jesus says, 'only to the lost sheep of the house of Israel' (v. 24). Although non-Israelites were to be blessed and favoured by Jesus, and although the final commission to the church was that she should go into all the world, it was true that Jesus was sent to Israel, to live and preach among those people to whom God had committed his law and his covenant from the beginning.

When the woman then begs for his help, Jesus raises a third barrier: 'It is not right to take the children's bread and throw it to the dogs' (v. 26). As a Gentile, that is how she was viewed. 'Dogs' is a word that Jesus has already used in the Sermon on the Mount (7:6) and one that Paul will use of the enemies of the cross (Phil. 3:2). Her response is superb: even dogs can eat crumbs. She was willing to stoop down to receive the blessing, even to the lowest level.

Jesus has subjected her to a threefold test: the first, a test of the sincerity of her desire; the second, a test of its intensity; the third, a test of her own integrity. Her faith triumphs at last, and her daughter is healed.

Such scenes as these illustrate and anticipate the fact that the blessings of Jesus will indeed extend beyond the people of Israel to the Gentiles of every land.

The King and the sick and hungry (15:29–39)

Reactions of the crowd to Jesus are registered in Matthew's brief summary of the continuing healing ministry of the Lord. Again we find Jesus on a mountain (v. 29), and again we find crowds coming to him. People with a variety of conditions come to Jesus, and he is able to restore and heal. His word and touch make such a difference in these lives.

The result is that 'they glorified the God of Israel' (v. 31). We cannot ignore the Old Testament overtones in this designation. The God of the Old Testament is the God of the New, and it is this God who reveals himself to us in Jesus Christ. The miracles were not simply worked to attract people's interest, or even to alleviate their need, pain and distress; they were performed in order that God might have glory among those who received the benefit and blessing of his power and nearness.

The miracles continue with another instance of Jesus feeding a large crowd. This time, Jesus takes the initiative himself, declaring his compassion for them; and once again, he feeds them by multiplying a few loaves and a few fish. Again there is an abundance left over; and again the number is given—four thousand, as opposed to the five thousand of 14:21.

Some scholars have suggested that Matthew is simply recounting the same incident here, although it is difficult to work out why he would do that. Some have argued that the feeding of the five thousand took place on Jewish territory and the feeding of the four thousand on Gentile territory. Others suggest that the two events parallel the miracles of Elijah and Elisha.

But why not accept the obvious? One of the early church fathers, St John Chrysostom, put it like this:

> But why at the former time, when there were five thousand, did twelve baskets full remain over and above, whereas here, when there were four thousand, it was seven baskets full? For what purpose, I say, and by what cause, were the remnants less, the guests not being so many?
>
> Either then one may say this, that the baskets on this last occasion were greater than those used before, or if this were not so, lest the equality of the miracle should again cast them into forgetfulness. He rouses their recollection by the difference, that by the variation they might be reminded of both one and the other. Accordingly, in that case, He makes the baskets full of fragments equal in number to His disciples; in this, the other baskets equal to the loaves; indicating even hereby his unspeakable power, and the ease wherewith He exercised His authority, in that it was possible for Him to work such miracles, both in this way and in the other.
>
> For neither was it of small power, to maintain the exact number, both then and now, then when there were five thousand, now when there were four thousand, and not suffer the remnants to be more than the baskets used on the one occasion or on the other, although the number of the guests was different.[4]

In other words, the differences in the details can be explained as a way by which Jesus reminded the people of his great power and of the fact that he was under no constraints in the exercise of his ability. The same compassion was equal to any situation, and the same power was in exercise in a variety of different circumstances.

The King and the religious leaders (again!) (16:1–12)

Once again, Matthew injects a note of hostility and confrontation. The more Jesus' fame grows, and the more the crowds gather to him and experience his healing touch and his compassionate provision, the more the opposition grows. We know that he is the anointed one, the true, legitimate King of God's choosing. But there is another kingdom in the world, one which is in opposition to the kingdom of God. The sad thing is that it is often dressed up in religion.

The Pharisees come to test him (v. 1), asking him to show them a sign. The Greek word translated 'test' can also mean 'tempt', and it is this Greek word that Matthew used of Jesus' temptations in chapter 4. The opposition is growing and is now coming from the religious leaders. They know about Jesus' miracles; they want him to perform one just for them.

Jesus' answer is very simple. People understand the significance of things every day: a red sky at night is the sign of good weather to come; a red sky in the morning is the sign of bad weather. How is it possible, Jesus asks, for people to read the skies but not the signs of the times?

Jesus accuses his opponents of spiritual adultery. Instead of being content with the signs God has already given, they want more. Jesus tells them that they ought to be satisfied with the sign of Jonah. Although the bare reference is enigmatic, we should probably link this back to 12:38–41, where the significance of Jonah—again in response to the Pharisees' request for a sign—is more expansively given.

Jonah was in the earth for three days and three nights; so Jesus will be 'in the heart of the earth' (12:40) for the same period.

Jesus is telling them to read what is there in Scripture and is obvious. C. S. Lewis wrote a famous essay on 'Fern Seed and Elephants', in which he talked about people claiming to see the significance of the smallest things while not seeing the elephants in front of them. Jesus is saying that the Pharisees are like that—unwilling to accept the clearest revelation from God.

As a result of this encounter, Jesus gives a warning to the disciples in which he not only explicitly highlights the evil of the Pharisees, but also draws out the significance of the miracle with the bread and fish. He describes the religion of the Pharisees as 'leaven', or 'yeast'. One of the most significant elements of the act of redemption by which God took his people out of the land of Egypt concerned unleavened bread:

> In the first month, from the fourteenth day of the month at evening, you shall eat unleavened bread until the twenty-first day of the month at evening. For seven days no leaven is to be found in your houses. If anyone eats what is leavened, that person will be cut off from the congregation of Israel, whether he is a sojourner or a native of the land. You shall eat nothing leavened; in all your dwelling places you shall eat unleavened bread (Exod. 12:18–20).

Subsequent Old Testament laws also demanded an absence of yeast—the grain offering, for example, was not to be baked with leaven (Lev. 6:17). Paul sees this as significant for Christian holiness:

> Do you not know that a little leaven leavens the whole lump? Cleanse out the old leaven that you may be a new lump, as you really are unleavened. For Christ, our Passover lamb, has been sacrificed. Let us therefore celebrate the festival, not with the old leaven, the leaven of malice and evil, but with the unleavened bread of sincerity and truth (1 Cor. 5:6–8).

So when Jesus mentions leaven, the disciples think he is speaking about bread. 'We have brought no bread,' they say. Jesus' response is obvious: have they not seen nor remembered the miracles? He can produce bread any time! The leaven he is talking about is not yeast for baking but 'the teaching of the Pharisees and Sadducees', which has the power to influence our lives and affect our behaviour. We need to make sure that the religion of the Pharisees does not become our religion.

The King and the confessing church (16:13–20)

This section of Matthew's Gospel comes to a close with an important conversation between Jesus and his disciples in Caesarea Philippi. Jesus does several things:

First, he asks about the opinions among people as to his own identity (v. 13). The disciples convey for us the differing attitudes to Jesus which were evident among the people. For some, like Herod, Jesus was the reincarnation of John the Baptist; others identified him as one of the great classical prophets, like Jeremiah or Elijah. Different views of Jesus abounded then, and they abound still.

Second, he directs the question to the disciples (v. 15). What is their opinion of him? It is the direct question 'But who do you say that I am?' that elicits the supremely important confession of faith on the part of Peter: 'You are the Christ, the Son of the living God' (v. 16). There is possibly no greater statement in the whole of this Gospel; it is to this point that Jesus has been bringing the disciples, gradually opening their eyes to his messianic glory so that their mouths might be opened to confess him as the anointed one of God. The public ministry of Jesus began with the Father's acknowledgement 'This is my beloved Son' (3:17), and on Jesus' own authority we know that no one knows the Son except the Father (11:27). But the disciples had come to know him, too, and to trust in him.

To confess Jesus as Son of God, therefore, is to go higher still; it is to say that Jesus is more than a man and more than the Messiah: he is God himself.

So when Jesus asks, 'Who is the Son of Man?' Peter answers, 'He is the Son of God!' The title 'Son of Man' is not merely a description of humanness; it is a title of the Messiah. To confess Jesus as Son of God, therefore, is to go higher still; it is to say that Jesus is more than a man and more than the Messiah: he is God himself. 'It would seem to imply that in and through Jesus God has manifested himself as the God who imparts life, and that in the manifestation and transmission of this life of God, Jesus has shown Himself the veritable Son of God, partaking of the life and life-giving character of God Himself.'[5]

Jesus tells Peter that such a confession can only come by

revelation; in the same way that only the Son can reveal the Father (11:27), so only the Father can reveal the Son (16:17). Now we see how Matthew contrasts his subjects so effectively. God hides the mysteries of the gospel from the wise and reveals them to children (11:25); in this chapter, the Pharisees represent the 'wise' from whom these mysteries are hidden, while Peter is one of the 'little children' who receive the revelation from God.

Third, Jesus sets out his purpose and plan (vv. 18–19). There is a play here on the name 'Peter', which means 'a stone'; Jesus says that there is a rock on which Jesus is going to build his church. These words have been interpreted and misinterpreted down through the years. The Roman Catholic Church, for example, has always insisted that Peter was the rock on which the church was to be built, although within a very short time Satan was to use Peter's voice to rebuke Jesus (16:23).

It is more natural to understand Jesus' purpose as being to build his church, not on the disciple, but on his confession: the basis of the church is that Jesus is confessed as Lord. It is through the church that Christ intends to make his word and will known; when she speaks in Christ's name, the church binds and looses, and opens the gates of heaven to those who believe and closes them on those who do not.

Fourth, Jesus asks the disciples to keep these things secret for the moment (v. 20). That strikes us as odd; why should Jesus not wish the world to know his identity? Part of the answer is that the time would come when people would indeed have the glory of Christ preached to them; but that time had not yet come.

For further study ▶

FOR FURTHER STUDY

1. Matthew tells us that Jesus fed the five thousand out of compassion (14:14). In what contexts does Jesus show compassion in the following passages: Mark 6:34; 9:22; Luke 7:13? God is said to have compassion in Deuteronomy 30:3; 2 Chronicles 36:15; and Isaiah 49:13. What do these passages teach us about the nature of God?
2. Compare Peter's actions in Matthew 14:28–32 with his actions in John 21:4–8. Can you highlight any differences in these incidents? What had Peter learned between times?
3. What is the contrast between 14:31 and 15:28? What are the differences in the two types of faith?
4. In 15:31, Matthew uses the phrase 'the God of Israel'. How do the following passages use this designation: Joshua 7:19; 8:30; 24:23; 1 Kings 8:15; Psalm 59:5; Isaiah 29:23; Luke 1:68?
5. Hypocrisy is compared to leaven, or yeast, in 16:6–12. What do the following passages say about leaven: Exodus 12:15; 1 Corinthians 5:8?

TO THINK ABOUT AND DISCUSS

1. In Romans 9:15, Paul quotes the following words: 'I will have compassion on whom I have compassion.' What do they mean? Why does Paul cite them?
2. What does it mean to have 'little faith' (14:31). Do you ever have 'little faith'?
3. Is tradition always bad (see 15:3)? Explain your answer.
4. How can we guard against hypocrisy in our lives?

Part 3—The King destroys his enemy

(16:21–28:20)

'Behold, your king is coming to you, humble, and mounted on a donkey ...' (Matt. 21:5)

8 The King reveals his glory

(16:21–17:27)

It's not just on a human level that Jesus interacts with others; we are reminded that Satan has his opinion of him, and that God has his opinion, too. When some refuse to listen to the voice of the King, God bids us hear him.

The enemy of the King (16:21–28)

Just as the account of the first phase of the public ministry of Jesus was marked by the words 'From that time …' in 4:17, so the beginning of the next is marked in 16:21. Jesus now shows that the end for which he has come into the world is to suffer, die and then rise again. This becomes the main theme of his preaching from this time onwards.

However, Peter, who has just confessed Jesus as the Son of God, does not like this new note that is now predominant in Jesus' preaching. Peter does not want to think of Jesus being crucified and he rebukes him for saying such things (v. 22).

Jesus immediately confronts the situation by addressing, not Peter, but Satan: he recognizes that the voice that has been speaking to him has been the voice of the one he has come to destroy. He is not unfamiliar with the voice; he heard it in the temptation at the beginning (ch. 4). Now he hears it again; only, this time, one of the disciples is the mouthpiece of the enemy.

'Get behind me, Satan!' is a powerful word for the moment. It is interesting that he does not say, 'Get behind me, Peter!' In a sense, Jesus is separating Peter and Satan—Peter is in front of him, even as Satan is behind him.

Coupled with the rebuke of Satan and the chastising of Peter is the call to the life of discipleship as a life of cross-bearing. The followers of Jesus must deny themselves, take up the cross and follow him (v. 24). He is going to take up his cross and follow the will of the Father; his people must walk in his steps. As John Piper puts it, 'Even before heaven, joy abounds along the hard road that leads through death to resurrection. Nothing can compare with the joy of walking in the light with Jesus as opposed to walking in the darkness without him.'[1]

Jesus demands a life of cross-bearing, of constant dying, because he offers something better than the best the world can give. There is a future when the Son of Man will appear in his glory and repay each person (v. 27). That prospect is what makes the cross here worthwhile.

And yet, some were to catch a glimpse of that glory on another of Matthew's great mountains …

The glory of the King (17:1–13)

The transfiguration account is paralleled in the other

Synoptic Gospels (Mark 9:2–8; Luke 9:28–36) and it clearly had a profound effect on those who witnessed it. Peter draws our attention to it in 2 Peter 1:16, and John's statement that 'we have seen his glory' (John 1:14) must include the transfiguration.

In this passage, there are clear echoes of Old Testament theophany (a theophany is an appearance of God), not least the appearance of God on Mount Sinai. In Exodus 24, for example, God invites Moses, Aaron, Aaron's sons and seventy elders to come up the mountain to him. The people do not go up. On the mountain, the glory of the God of Israel is revealed: '... they saw the God of Israel. There was under his feet as it were a pavement of sapphire stone, like the very heaven for clearness' (Exod. 24:10).

In a similar manner, now Jesus takes three representatives of his covenant people to a mountain, where his appearance is transformed to the extent that his native, divine splendour radiates through his clothes and in his face. Three things highlight the glory of Jesus at this point.

The transformation of his appearance (v. 2)

Jesus' face shines 'like the sun'. Interestingly, when Moses was in the presence of God, his face shone with a reflected glory that was so great that he had to cover his face in the presence of the Israelites (Exod. 34:30). Jesus possesses that glory himself. It has been eclipsed and veiled by his bodily appearance, but on the mount of transfiguration, the veil is lifted.

His clothes also become 'white as light', not because of a light shining on him from the outside but because of the light shining out of him from the inside. Just as the appearance of

God in Exodus 24 is accompanied by a jewelled pavement like heaven itself, so the whiteness of Jesus' clothes is beyond anything that earth can accomplish (Mark 9:3).

The company of Moses and Elijah (vv. 3–4)

We do not read that their faces are shining or that their clothes are white; even in this exalted company, Jesus stands supreme. Yet the appearance of these long-departed saints adds to the lustre of Jesus. So here, on this one mountain, is the first author of Scripture (Moses), the last author of Scripture (John) and the one of whom the Scriptures speak: Jesus himself.

It is a common approach to view Moses and Elijah as representing the Law and the Prophets, which Jesus declares in the Sermon on the Mount he is fulfilling (5:17). Interestingly, both Moses and Elijah are mentioned in the closing verses of the Old Testament prophetic literature: 'Remember the law of my servant Moses, the statutes and rules that I commanded him at Horeb for all Israel. Behold, I will send you Elijah the prophet before the great and awesome day of the LORD comes' (Mal. 4:4–5). Also, in this part of Matthew's Gospel, Elijah is mentioned several times: in 16:14, Peter tells us that some people consider Jesus to be Elijah; and in 17:10–13, Jesus clarifies the fact that the prophecy regarding the coming of Elijah is fulfilled in John the Baptist's ministry.

By appearing with Moses and Elijah, therefore, Jesus is clearly distinguished from them both. But why these particular saints? Let's state the obvious about them:

- They were both Old Testament men. Indeed, they were the

last named men in the prophetic books of the Bible (Mal. 4:4–5). At the most basic level, the story of Moses and Elijah is the story of Christ, continuous with all previous revelation and redemptive history. Christ represents a new chapter in the same book, not a new book.

- They were both Old Testament prophets. Moses represents Law only because he was a prophet. He was not the first prophet of the Bible, but there was no prophet like him (Deut. 34:10–11). He eclipses even Elijah. Yet with Elijah we find the resumption of prophetic ministry after a long period of silence. And it is the apostle Peter who tells us that the spirit of Jesus runs through the prophetic ministry of the Old Testament (1 Peter 1:10–11).
- They were both Old Testament prophets who performed signs and wonders. None of the great classical prophets such as Isaiah or Jeremiah performed miracles. But Moses did (Deut. 34:11), when the plagues came on Egypt; and so did Elijah, when through him God made continuous provision for a widow and then raised her son (1 Kings 17:8–24). In Elijah's case, the miracles served to show that the word of the Lord in his mouth was the truth (1 Kings 17:24). These miracles, therefore, authenticated Moses and Elijah as the messengers of God. The miracles of Jesus do the same. They do not serve to show us that we may perform signs and wonders today; rather, they demonstrate that these prophets received the stamp of authenticity from God.
- They were both Old Testament prophets who spoke with God and saw his glory on a mountain. God brought Moses back to Mount Sinai and spoke to him there face to face. Hiding him in a cave, he revealed his 'back' as his

glory passed by (Exod. 33:21–23). When Elijah was threatened by the queen, he came to Horeb, the mount of God, the same mountain as Sinai, and looked for a (Moses'?) cave, where the phenomena of Sinai appeared—wind, earthquake and fire—but where the presence of God came in a still voice. Similarly, at the transfiguration, the glory of God in the face of Christ is manifested, but it is a voice from heaven that directs the apostles to look alone to Jesus.

- They were both Old Testament prophets whose graves cannot be identified—Moses, because God buried him in an unknown location; and Elijah, because he did not have one.

They represent therefore, not so much the Law and the Prophets as the whole prophetic trajectory of the Old Testament, which is about to yield to the finality and glory of the prophet like Moses who will ascend into heaven like Elijah. Having spoken in former days to the fathers by the prophets in many different ways, God is now going to give us his Son, and he is going to say to us: 'Hear him.'

Peter's response, according to most translations, is '… it is good that we are here' (17:4), coupled with the suggestion to make tents for the three supernatural persons who appear on the mountain. It is difficult, however, to see how such a terrifying ordeal can lead to the desire to stay; all three accounts highlight the motive of fear that leads to speech born in ignorance (see 17:6; Mark 9:6; Luke 9:33). It may well be that he is asking a question: 'Is it good to be here?' For Peter, with his understanding of the Old Testament, the tabernacle is the place where God's glory can be domesticated so that God can dwell among his people. The response and the longing to construct tabernacles then becomes understandable: Peter does not wish to be exposed to the consuming glory of God—he wants to ensure that the glory will be contained in tabernacles, just as the glory revealed at Mount Sinai was.

The voice from heaven (v. 5)

Just as at Jesus' baptism, there is a voice that speaks from the glory, out of a cloud, saying, 'This is my beloved Son, with whom I am well pleased; listen to him.' This voice echoes 3:17, but develops our understanding further, as we realize that the beloved Son is the prophet who was to come into the world. The voice from heaven, therefore, serves to show that Jesus is one with the prophetic tradition represented by Moses and Elijah, but that he is also the consummator of that tradition. He is, in fact, the last prophet.

The voice from heaven, therefore, serves to show that Jesus is one with the prophetic tradition represented by Moses and Elijah, but that he is also the consummator of that tradition. He is, in fact, the last prophet.

The descent from the mount of transfiguration serves to highlight other issues. The true meaning of Elijah's appearance is emphasized by Jesus as he identifies Elijah with John the Baptist (vv. 9–13). Jesus still wishes the disciples to keep the events they have witnessed secret. The time for proclamation and publication will come, but is not yet. The unexplained question lingers in the minds of the disciples—why is the coming of Elijah a matter of rabbinic teaching? Jesus' answer is that the prophecy concerning the coming of Elijah was fulfilled in the appearance of John. And just as Elijah and John were cruelly mistreated in the world, so, too, will Jesus be.

Further glimpses of glory (17:14–27)

The glory of the King is seen in the healing of the epileptic boy (vv. 14–21). This is where the real battle is fought—not on the mountain top of blessing and privilege but in the valley of sickness and demon-possession. There is no need to argue that the identification of epilepsy with demon-possession is the sign of pre-modern science; Matthew's record demonstrates that, in this case, the epilepsy had more than a physical cause and therefore needed to be dealt with by spiritual means. Once again, the 'little faith' of the disciples is highlighted.

The glory of the King is, however, eclipsed by suffering, humiliation and obedience (vv. 22–23). Jesus is the one to suffer and die. He also shows his willingness to submit to earthly authority, by making arrangements for paying the temple tax (vv. 24–27). This incident, like the confession at Caesarea Philippi and the transfiguration, particularly involves Peter. Matthew, the tax collector, has an obvious interest in it (see also 22:15–22), and we should see it as part of Jesus' concern to uphold the civil power, even if the taxes imposed were less than equitable and just. Submission is to be the mark of Jesus' ministry from this time forward. The glorious King is also a glorious Servant.

For further study ▶

FOR FURTHER STUDY

1. Jesus promised to give Peter 'the keys of the kingdom of heaven' (16:19). How do the following passages enable us to understand this better: Isaiah 22:22; John 20:23; Revelation 1:18; 3:7?
2. Both Moses and Elijah spoke with God on top of a mountain. Can you find points of comparison and of contrast between Moses on Sinai in Exodus 24 and Elijah on Horeb (= Sinai) in 1 Kings 19? How do these passages relate to the transfiguration passage?
3. Read 2 Peter 1:16–17. What was the significance to Peter of the transfiguration? How might the transfiguration experience have led John to write the words of John 1:14?

TO THINK ABOUT AND DISCUSS

1. What is the rock of Matthew 16:18? Do you think it is Peter? Or his confession? Does this shed light for us on the importance of publicly professing Christ?
2. What are the terms of discipleship according to 16:24–25? Many of the early Christians were literally crucified. What might it mean for us today to 'take up the cross'? What might it mean for you to 'lose your life' in order to be Christ's disciple?
3. Was the transfiguration for Jesus' benefit? Or for the benefit of the disciples? Or both? Is it necessary for us to have a great experience of the glory of Jesus in order to have faith in him as Son of God?

9 The King teaches his church

(18:1–20:34)

By the standards of the world, Jesus was not great. But only he knew, and taught, the secret of true greatness. As Head of the church, he reminds us of what true greatness is and encourages us to follow his example. In this section, we listen once again to the wisdom of the King.

The fourth major block of teaching in Matthew's Gospel has to do with the nature of kingdom life. The teaching section is in chapter 18 and, characteristically, the material that follows it begins with the phrase 'Now when Jesus had finished these sayings …' (19:1). However, the activity of chapters 19–20 is of a piece with the teaching of chapter 18, and these chapters together show us the wisdom of Jesus Christ, the great royal Prophet and prophetic King.

Greatness in the kingdom (18:1–14)

The question asked by the disciples in 18:1—'Who is the greatest in the kingdom of heaven?'—might be appropriate in an earthly, worldly kingdom but is far from honourable in the kingdom of heaven. In spite of the fact that the King himself has made it clear he is to take the path of submission, suffering and death, his disciples are still thinking in terms of grandeur and reward.

Jesus overturns their thinking by showing them that belonging to the kingdom is conditional on our becoming like children. We can only truly belong to the kingdom of God when we come to him in weakness, dependence and need. We cannot enter the kingdom of heaven in our own strength and self-sufficiency.

So important is this to Jesus that he defends those who live kingdom lives as children of God from any assault on them. His language in verse 6 is strong: '… whoever causes one of these little ones who believe in me to sin, it would be better for him to have a great millstone fastened around his neck and to be drowned in the depth of the sea.' The path to greatness in the kingdom of heaven is through humility and self-emptying, and those who take this position are those whom Christ calls his own and promises to defend.

Jesus also makes it clear that living such a life as he demands is rewarding precisely because it is all-encompassing. The world presents his people with temptations to sin, but his call to us is to overcome and to defeat sin. If we really believe in eternal fire and in suffering beyond the grave, we will do everything to ensure that we enjoy the eternal life he promises his people.

The parable of the lost sheep (vv. 10–14) echoes the telling of it in Luke 15:4–7, although the purpose of it here is different. The value of the one sheep for whom the shepherd searches is what makes it important for us to guard our relations with other members of his kingdom. If the Father has searched for the sheep, and the angels guard the children of the kingdom, then we should do our utmost to protect them.

Forgiveness in the kingdom (18:15–35)

Our belonging to Christ's kingdom, therefore, has profound implications, not only for the way we relate to God, but also for the way we relate to one another. Christ has made it clear that we are not to sin against other members of the household of faith. But how do we respond when they sin against us? That is the message of the remainder of the chapter. The first part of this fourth teaching block has shown how we should avoid offending our brothers and sisters; the second concerns how we should deal with them when they offend us.

So, what should we do if our brother sins against us? Jesus sets four principles before us.

Principle 1: Go and tell him his fault (v. 15)

There is no virtue in harbouring grudges, and precious little time afforded to us for keeping grudges alive. According to Jesus, 'It's good to talk', and the first thing we need to do when dealing with an errant brother is to speak with him. If he listens to us, and the matter is resolved between us, then, in the words of Jesus, we have 'gained' our brother.

Principle 2: Take others and go and speak to him (v. 16)

It may be that, in spite of our efforts to effect a peaceful reconciliation, our brother does not listen to us at a face-to-face meeting. The second step is to take others along. The Old Testament principle was that evidence in court would stand if the testimony of two or three witnesses agreed (Deut. 19:15). It is good practice to have these personal issues dealt with in the same way, so that others can corroborate our version of events.

Principle 3: Tell the church (v. 17)

If going to the erring brother does not work, Jesus tells us to bring the matter to the church. This is the second time Matthew has used the concept of the church (the first was at 16:18) and it shows that, for Matthew, there is an important relationship between the concept of Christian discipleship and the concept of the church. The church as the fellowship of believers is the arena within which relationships between disciples should be fostered and corrected.

Principle 4: Excommunicate (v. 17)

Refusal to listen to the church is, according to Jesus, the last straw. To refuse the guidance of Christ in this way is to rebel against the God-appointed expression of authority in his kingdom. Jesus says that the brother who refuses the counsel of the church is to be regarded as 'a Gentile and a tax collector'; the latter phrase in particular would have resonated with Matthew.

The reason why Jesus is so insistent on this order of

procedure is precisely because he has given such authority to his people, and delegated to them the power to bind and loose. That does not mean that church authority always follows the will of Jesus, or that Jesus always acts the way the church determines. But it does show the high regard that Jesus has for the church, because it is the company where Christ is present and the Father is at work (18:19–20).

The remainder of the chapter may appear to contradict these principles, as Jesus emphasizes the importance of forgiveness and teaches that brothers who sin against us should be forgiven. But there is no contradiction: forgiveness does not mean ignoring the offence. Any expression of church 'discipline' is with a view to effecting forgiveness and restoring the erring party to fellowship.

The parable of the unforgiving servant illustrates this well (vv. 23–35). The king, settling his accounts, forgave a servant who owed him much. The forgiveness was motivated by pity and compassion. But then, when the servant met someone who was in debt to him to a much lesser degree, he began insisting on immediate payment. The king was appalled that one who had been forgiven should treat others contrary to how he himself had been treated.

We are, therefore, to give expression to our sense of wonder at having been forgiven precisely by forgiving those who have sinned against us (see 6:12,14–15).

Morality in the kingdom (19:1–30)

Jesus' teaching in Matthew 19 is in response to various questions put to him by the Pharisees (v. 3), by a rich young man (v. 16) and by the disciples (vv. 25,27). His answers to these questions continue the theme of kingdom lifestyle and behaviour which has been running through this Gospel.

The chapter is significant because it marks the end of Jesus' ministry in Galilee (v. 1), where Jesus has been preaching since the outset of his ministry. The change in direction will ultimately bring Jesus to the cross.

Several issues of ethics and morality are raised in this chapter.

Questions about divorce (vv. 1–15)

The Pharisees try to trip Jesus up in argument. They 'wanted to bring Jesus a test he couldn't pass'.[1] The subject of divorce was often fiercely debated between the rabbis, so to ask whether divorce was possible for absolutely any reason was a way of ensuring that whatever answer Jesus gave would be wrong in someone's estimation. The difficulty arose, not because the Old Testament law had nothing to say on the subject, but precisely because it was mentioned, for example, in Deuteronomy 24:1–4 (hence the reference to Moses in Matt. 19:7).

Jesus' first response to the question of whether divorce is ever a legitimate option in his view is to return to the foundational principles of marriage. Quoting from Genesis 2:24, Jesus reminds the Pharisees that marriage is as old as creation. Marriage was one of the provisions God made for man at the beginning of the world for his better enjoyment of and personal fulfilment in God's world. Even before sin came in to spoil and mar God's creation, it was not good that Adam was alone (Gen. 2:18). God provided a wife for him, with whom he could enjoy a reciprocal and mutual relationship of love. The fact that God ordained this to take place in an exclusive relationship of marriage means that marriage is rightly termed a 'creation ordinance'.

Jesus' view of marriage is clearly stated in verse 6: '... they are no longer two but one flesh. What therefore God has joined together let not man separate.' We must always begin our discussion of divorce with the biblical principle of marriage.

The Pharisees then rein in with the obvious question: 'If this is the case, why does Moses concede the possibility of divorce?' Jesus' answer is that the law of Deuteronomy 24 was necessary because of the 'hardness of heart' on the part of the people. It was, in other words, a law designed, not to make divorce quick and easy, but to make it a last resort in extreme circumstances. The intention of the law was to give time to consider the implications of annulling a marriage. Without it, people might simply walk away from marriage commitments. Jesus explains that Moses' law was no contradiction of the creation ordinance, but rather a way of protecting it.

This is made even clearer by the insistence that divorce ought only to be contemplated on the grounds of sexual immorality, which involves marital unfaithfulness; otherwise the marriage is not over and remarriage is adultery. So the answer to the first question is 'Yes, divorce can be a legitimate option'; but the answer to the second question is 'Only on the grounds of adultery and unfaithfulness should divorce be contemplated.'

The standard taught by Jesus, therefore, is 'chastity before marriage, fidelity after marriage, and a lifelong commitment of one married partner to the other with no thought of divorce'.[2] No wonder the disciples say that 'it is better not to marry'! But Jesus does not agree with them. All he means is that it will not be everyone's lot to marry. Some—like Jesus himself—live lives of celibacy and perpetual virginity. Without the cares and responsibilities of marriage and family life, Jesus, like John the Baptist before him, was celibate for the sake of the kingdom. But for those who do enter into marriage, the blessings are to be enjoyed in proportion to the standards being met.[3]

The incident with the children (vv. 13–15) again illustrates the childlike nature of kingdom life. By blessing the children, Jesus shows himself to be interested in all levels of society. The disciples, who think Jesus is too busy to devote time to children, receive his rebuke and have to learn again that the kingdom of heaven belongs to such as they.

Questions about the commandments (vv. 16–22)

Another question triggers further discussion about the Law. It comes from an unidentified young man who asks Jesus about doing good things to enter the kingdom. While modern evangelists might present this man with the gospel in six easy steps, Jesus' response seems designed to turn him away. Jesus refers to the commandments, explicitly mentioning the sixth, seventh, eighth, ninth, fifth and tenth laws of the Decalogue (in that order) but implying the continued authority of all ten. Keeping these commandments is the way to 'enter life' (v. 17).

The young man has prided himself with having done exactly that. Thinking he has nothing more to do, he asks

Jesus what is lacking in his life. Jesus' response to him is that he should sell all his goods and give them to the poor, and then he should follow Jesus. The young man fails the test; instead of responding positively to Jesus' words, he goes away sorrowful.

Jesus was not advocating the selling of our possessions as an absolute condition for entering the kingdom. If he were, he would have said this to everyone, and there would be no rich believers in the Bible. Rather, he was using this to expose the true nature of the young man's heart; although, like Paul, he was blameless in his law-keeping (see Phil. 3:6), he was still a slave to materialism and his many possessions. His life might have been morally exemplary, but his heart was not in love with God.

It is always important to remind ourselves that, even in the Old Testament, commandment-keeping and loving God went side by side.

It is always important to remind ourselves that, even in the Old Testament, commandment-keeping and loving God went side by side. So Moses says in Deuteronomy 11:1, 'You shall therefore love the LORD your God and keep his charge, his statutes, his rules, and his commandments always.' The condition which Jesus imposed on the young man of this chapter showed that his claim always to have kept all the commandments was contradicted by the fact that he loved things more than he loved God.

Questions about what God's kingdom offers (vv. 23–30)

The incident with the young man raises the issue of wealth. Jesus suggests that it is difficult, though not impossible, for a rich person to enter God's kingdom. Jesus compares it to bringing a camel through the eye of a needle. Only by God's intervention, grace and power is such a feat possible. Naturally speaking, it would be entirely impossible, and foolish even to try.

Peter interjects (again). 'We have left everything and followed you,' he says to Jesus in verse 27. 'What then will we have?'

Jesus' response to this question raises the horizon of Peter's sights and vision to a 'new world' that will be revealed when the Son of Man appears in his glory. Although Peter has seen Jesus in glory in the transfiguration, that is just a small glimpse of the glory to be revealed at the end, when Jesus comes again. These verses anticipate the final block of teaching in chapters 24–25.

Jesus' answer to Peter shows that it is no loss to have given up everything to follow Jesus. There may be difficulty and suffering, even persecution and death, involved in belonging to Jesus' kingdom, but the losses will be made good—those who follow him will receive a hundred times as much as they lost, along with eternal life. On the other hand, those who thought they could gain the world as well as their souls will be disappointed.

Serving in the kingdom (20:1–34)

The phrase '[the] first will be last, and the last first', which occurs at the end of chapter 19, recurs in 19:16, linking this section with what has gone before. The King continues to speak as one whose glory is revealed in service. There are three aspects to kingdom service brought before us here.

Those who serve receive the same wage (vv. 1–16)

The parable of the labourers in the vineyard highlights for us the fact that any investment we make in the work of the kingdom of heaven receives its reward, and that the reward is the same for everyone. In the parable, the same wages are distributed to those who have worked all day long, those who have worked half a day and those who have worked for just a few hours at the end of the day.

In the parable, some grumble at this arrangement, but the master who hired the workers says, 'I am doing you no wrong.'

Lying behind the parable is the thought that we serve in the kingdom of heaven not so much for the reward we receive as for our delight in the service itself. Do we serve willingly and gladly, simply because we love our Lord and Master?

Jesus serves by giving his life (vv. 17–28)

In this matter of service, as in every other matter, Jesus himself is our supreme example. Having already predicted his death by betrayal, condemnation and crucifixion in 16:21–23 and 17:22–23, he here predicts it again for a third time. Obviously, the cross is looming large now in his vision and all that is taking place in the Gospel is moving Jesus closer to the point of his death.

It is all the more incongruous, therefore, that 'the mother of the sons of Zebedee'—that is, the mother of James and John—should request of Jesus that he grant a special place of honour and privilege in his kingdom to her sons. Clearly, the teaching of Jesus regarding the nature of the kingdom is still being warped by a worldly idea of kingdom life. He is not offering political power and glory but rather a spiritual kingdom that may involve suffering here and now. Indeed, only as Christ's followers are able to drink Jesus' cup of suffering can they share in Christ's glory (v. 22; see also 26:39).

The disciples as a body needed to learn that the way to greatness in Christ's kingdom is by humility and service, after the example of the Son of Man, who came to serve.

Only through Jesus' service can we receive benefit and healing (20:29–34)

The words about the Son of Man in verse 28 are quickly followed by a description of Jesus as Son of David (v. 30), as two blind men call on the Son of David to have mercy on them. This brings together some of the threads of the Gospel narrative. Jesus has been heralded as the Son of David from the beginning; he is also the Son of Man who is to suffer, and it is to him that we must come for healing and for salvation. His miraculous touch restores sight to the blind, a further indication of his messianic and prophetic ministry.

FOR FURTHER STUDY

1. Compare the versions of the story of the lost sheep in 18:10–14 and Luke 15:4–7. Does the story have the same purpose in the two accounts?
2. What does Jesus tell us to tell to the church in 18:17? Does 1 Corinthians 5:4–5 represent an application of the principles Jesus is teaching?
3. Jesus talks about forgiveness in 18:22. What is forgiveness? Can forgiveness happen without repentance? What is the relationship between the teaching here in Matthew and the teaching of Jesus in Luke 17:1–4?
4. In 19:17, Jesus says to the young man, '… keep the commandments'. How does Romans 13:8–10 relate to this theme?
5. Read 20:22. What cup did Jesus have to drink? Compare this with 26:39–42.

TO THINK ABOUT AND DISCUSS

1. What are the issues that the subject of divorce raises for the church today? Can the Bible help us to decide when divorce is permitted and when it is not?
2. In the light of 19:21, should we sell our possessions?
3. How do you understand Jesus' phrase '[the] first will be last, and the last first' (19:30 and 20:16)?

10 The King journeys to his city

(21:1–11)

Jesus enters Jerusalem, which is where the great drama of redemption will be enacted. We are now entering the final movements of the ministry. Indeed, we are entering the final week of Jesus' public ministry, in which, as Craig Blomberg says, 'anticipation and conflict both grow to a fever pitch'.[1] This so-called 'triumphal entry' is the beginning of the end of Jesus' public ministry.

Of course, as in the other Gospels, the narrative of the last days of Jesus' earthly life occupies proportionally more space than that of the preceding three years. Every effort is made by the Gospel writers to demonstrate and highlight the overriding significance of the Passion, death and resurrection of the Lord. These are the events that lie at the heart of the gospel.

The journey of the King (21:1–11)

Jesus sends two disciples for a donkey and a colt, commandeering their use for his own processional approach to and entry into the city. As he sits on the animals, the crowds lining the streets spread branches and cloaks on the road and sing 'Hosanna' to him.

This entry into Jerusalem is significant for several reasons.

It fulfils biblical prophecy (vv. 4–5)

Matthew cites Zechariah 9:9: 'Rejoice greatly, O daughter of Zion! Shout aloud, O daughter of Jerusalem! behold, your king is coming to you; righteous and having salvation is he, humble and mounted on a donkey, on a colt, the foal of a donkey.' John, in his Gospel, cites the same prophecy in his account of the entry into Jerusalem (John 12:15).

The passage in Zechariah is set in the context of judgement on the enemies of Israel and God's promise to build up and save his people. The messianic King will appear, and his kingdom will ultimately stretch 'from sea to sea, and from the River to the ends of the earth' (Zech. 9:10).

By quoting the prophecy, Matthew enables us to see one small part of the realization of God's redemptive purpose. The prophet gives a sweeping vision, which takes in the whole of history. Now, at the point in time in which Jesus enters the city, part of the prediction is fulfilled and the prophecy takes a step forward. This is consonant with Matthew's theme of the advent of the King.

It is also important to note, as Alistair Wilson points out, that 'the words found on the lips of the crowds in Matthew 21:9 are exactly reproduced in 23:39 on the lips of Jesus. They are a citation of Psalm 118:26 … Jesus sees a further enactment of the royal Psalm yet to come.'[2] The messianic theme 'reaches a new level of intensity'[3] in this section, as kingly qualities are applied to Jesus and he comes into his own city: the Son of David, regally entering the city of David.

It shows Jesus' humble obedience (v. 5)

Zechariah's prophecy declared that the King's appearance would be humble, and Matthew cites the full verse, including this note of humility. Interestingly, Jesus used the very same word about himself in Matthew 11:29, when he encouraged his followers to take up his yoke because he is 'gentle' and lowly.

> It is not merely riding on a donkey that makes Jesus humble. His very appearance in the world was a step of humility.

It is not merely riding on a donkey that makes Jesus humble. His very appearance in the world was a step of humility, and he has been taking such steps ever since, descending all the more into a situation of self-impoverishment and humility. In Paul's language, Jesus 'made himself nothing … he humbled himself by becoming obedient to the point of death' (Phil. 2:7–8). Nothing is more noteworthy than this: that the Jesus of all glory becomes the servant of no repute.

All of this is humility in the service of obedience. Jesus was the 'coming' one, the one whom God had commissioned to come into the world in order to bring salvation. Just as the Lord had need of the animal (21:3), so God had need of Jesus to ride it. He had commissioned his Son to come to Jerusalem and die. Although this event is often referred to as the 'triumphal entry', it was by way of betrayal, crucifixion and death that this King was to triumph over death for his people.

It highlights Jesus as both King and Prophet (vv. 8–11)

The crowds welcome Jesus as befits a king. But their answer to the question 'Who is this?' (v. 10) is 'This is the prophet Jesus, from Nazareth of Galilee.' Perhaps they are saying more than they realize; but what they are saying is the truth. Jesus has been commissioned by God both to declare the kingdom of heaven (as a prophet) and to inaugurate it (as a king).

By riding into the city in this way, Jesus is performing a prophetic, dramatic act, much like those of some of the Old Testament prophets.[4] Method and message combine as the enacted processional conveys the purposeful approach of Jesus to Jerusalem. While the crowds may expect that Jesus' aim is to overthrow Roman domination of Palestine, Matthew wants us to realize that there is a spiritual, rather than a political, significance to all of this.

Jesus' immediate purpose is to come into Jerusalem and die on a cross. But he makes it clear that his vision is long term and stretches out across history. His followers will take strength from his death and resurrection and will live to the end of the world in the light of his sovereign purpose.

For further study ▶

FOR FURTHER STUDY

1. Look at 21:1–11 in the light of the prophecy in Zechariah 9:9–17. Which elements of the prophecy were clearly fulfilled in the events that took place in Jerusalem?
2. The crowds say that Jesus is a prophet (21:11). How does he fulfil the prediction of a prophet like Moses given in Deuteronomy 18:15–22?

TO THINK ABOUT AND DISCUSS

1. What message do you think Jesus was giving as he rode into Jerusalem on a donkey? How does it illustrate Paul's point in Philippians 2:7, that Jesus 'made himself nothing'? How can we be like Jesus?
2. Why did the praises of the crowd so soon turn to shouts of 'Crucify him!' in 27:22–23? In the light of verses like Acts 2:23 and 1 Corinthians 2:7-8, how does the cross help us to understand the relationship between God's sovereignty and our responsibility? How would you answer this question: 'Was it right or wrong for Jesus to be crucified?'

11 The King predicts the future

(21:12–23:39)

In our study, we have focused on Jesus as the messianic King, but we have also noted that Matthew presents him as God's final Prophet. The actions and predictions of these next few chapters show Jesus to be the Prophet, in both word and deed, and highlight for us the King's authority.

While the chapters in this section of the Gospel record other dramatic prophetic acts (such as the cleansing of the temple and the cursing of the fig tree), they essentially demonstrate the authority of Jesus. Although much in this part of the Gospel will focus on future events, the text and its teaching are firmly rooted in past events. The section begins in 21:12 with Jesus entering the temple; in 24:1, he leaves the temple; and in 26:2, the final stages of Jesus' life are enacted around the Passover.

Old Testament sacred places and times run as recurring motifs through this part of the Gospel, and we are left in no doubt that this Jesus is the messianic King–Saviour whom God promised to send into the world. His authority is another recurring theme in this section. Jesus is asked, 'By what authority are you doing these things, and who gave you this authority?' (21:23). His teaching leaves men marvelling (22:22), astonished (22:33) and silent (22:46).

The King's authority displayed in action (21:12–22)

The authority of Jesus is displayed first by his clearing of the temple area and then by his cursing of the fig tree. The action in the temple is highly significant. As Jesus sees people buying and selling in the temple precincts, he is indignant. Instead of making the temple a place of worship, they have made it a 'den of robbers'.

By healing blind and lame people in the temple, Jesus shows how the temple ought to serve as a place of restoration and blessing. Children in the temple continue the chant of the crowd and sing 'Hosanna to the Son of David!' (v. 15). This angers the Jewish religious leaders, to whom Jesus responds with a citation from Psalm 8:2. A brief respite in Bethany follows.

For readers of the Gospels, this raises the question of how many temple cleansings there actually were. John records a similar incident at the *beginning* of Jesus' ministry (John 2:13–17). Was there just one such cleansing, placed by the Gospel writers at different points for literary or theological purposes? Or were there two? There does not seem to be any reason for us to deny the plain implication of the Gospel narratives: that Jesus cleansed the temple twice, once at the outset of his ministry—thus indicating the motive of honour for God which was to drive his ministry (John 2:17)—and again at its close, as he comes to honour his Father in his self-giving at Calvary.

One important consideration is the allusion to Zechariah in 21:5. By citing Zechariah 9:9 regarding the coming of the King, Matthew draws our attention to this important Old Testament prophet, whose latter prophecies focused on the coming day of the LORD. That day would be a day of salvation (Zech. 9:16). It would also be a day in which 'the glory of the house of David and the glory of the inhabitants of Jerusalem' (Zech. 12:8) would be made great, a day in which the inhabitants of Jerusalem would be cleansed from sin and uncleanness (Zech. 13:1) and in which the people would go to Jerusalem to worship the King (Zech. 14:16). Interestingly, the last statement of Zechariah is that 'there shall no longer be a trader in the house of the LORD of hosts on that day' (Zech. 14:21).[1]

The actions of Jesus, therefore, show him to be the expected messianic Saviour in the fullest sense. The ethical and spiritual uncleanness, represented both by the trading being pursued in the temple as well as by the disabilities which ordinarily bar access to the temple, will be overcome by the King. The cleansing of the temple thus becomes a symbol of the great work which he has come to accomplish.

The second symbolic action is the cursing of the fig tree. Jesus is hungry (v. 18) but finds no fruit on this tree. He pronounces a judgement on it, resulting in its immediate withering. Jesus' response to the disciples' question as to how this happened is to remind them of the importance of faith.

The fig tree is used in the Old Testament as a symbol of God's covenant blessing. Micah's vision of the future blessing of the mountain of the LORD, for example, includes the promise that 'they shall sit every man under his vine and under his fig tree, and no one shall make them afraid, for the mouth of the LORD of hosts has spoken' (Micah 4:4).

But Jeremiah also uses the image as a symbol of the sin of God's people. God says:

> When I would gather them, declares the LORD,
> there are no grapes on the vine,
> nor figs on the fig tree;
> even the leaves are withered,
> and what I gave them has passed away from them (Jer. 8:13).

Perhaps that is in Jesus' mind here: the fact that the fig tree is bearing no fruit is symbolic of the way in which God's people, in spite of their many blessings and privileges, have refused to listen to his voice or yield to his rule. When he might expect his fig tree to blossom, it is withered and decayed (see Luke 13:6–9).

The reference to prayer in verse 22 corresponds to Jesus' complaint about the temple in verse 13: prayer has been replaced by other matters of concern, and Jesus is drawing both his detractors and his disciples back to the basic principles of the faith.

The King's authority challenged (21:23–22:14)

Not surprisingly, these events continue to fuel the antagonism and enmity of the religious leaders. They question him directly as to the authority by which he is acting. Jesus' answer is a stroke of genius, as he refers them back to John (the Baptist) and to the authority that lay behind his practice. Jesus asks whether the authority was divine or human. The leaders know that if they affirm John's divine authority, Jesus can chide them for not believing him. If they deny John's divine authority, they run the risk of losing face with the crowd, who believe John to be a prophet. They simply cannot answer; and neither will Jesus answer their questions of him.

The conversation shows that, while they are ready to judge Jesus, they cannot even make a judgement about John. Their sin and moral impotence are exposed. They did not listen to what John taught; how shall they enter into dialogue with Jesus now? As the Puritan commentator Matthew Henry puts it: 'Those that imprison the truths they know ... are justly denied the further truths they enquire after.'[2]

The weakness of this challenge to the authority of Jesus is further exposed in three parables. Matthew appears to have set out his material very carefully at this point so that the three symbolic actions of entering Jerusalem are balanced by three significant parables, those of the two sons, the tenants and the wedding. As in chapter 13, Jesus takes situations that are common in the culture of the time and uses them to draw our attention to important matters.

Common to all three parables is the emphasis on the kingdom of God (21:31; 21:43; 22:2). Also common to all three is the underlying fact that some will enter the kingdom while others, who might have expected to enter, will not. This is the theme of this section of the Gospel. The opposition to Jesus comes not from the unbelieving world but from the religious elite, those whom Psalm 118:22

describes as 'builders' who have rejected the most important stone in the building.

These themes are highlighted in the three parables Matthew brings together here.

The parable of the two sons (21:28–32)

Here a man asks his sons to work in his vineyard. One son says he will not, but changes his mind and goes to work. The other son says he will do so, but does not. Similarly, those whom we expect to belong to the kingdom of God are the ones who are rejecting the Messiah. They refused to believe in John; now they are refusing to believe in Jesus.

The result is that entry into the kingdom of heaven will belong to those who appear on the surface to be the least likely candidates for it. As in the parable, so in 'real life': those who at first refused to listen to John's message and repent could have changed their minds later. It is their stubborn, persistent refusal to do so that now shuts them out of the kingdom even when others enter.

The parable of the tenants (21:33–46)

Like the previous parable, this one is also about a master commissioning work. In this case, tenants are put in charge of the man's vineyard and are commanded to look after it while he goes to live elsewhere. At harvest time, he sends a servant to examine the situation. The tenants maltreat all the servants sent to them for this reason, resorting to murder in one case. Eventually, the master sends his son, thinking that he will at least be shown reverence and respect. The tenants, however, reason that the death of the son will secure the inheritance for themselves, so they kill him. The consequence is that the master will return and exact vengeance from those who killed his son.

Matthew sheds light for us on the messianic implications of this parable by quoting from Psalm 118:22–23, in which builders reject the most important stone in a building. Those who have great privileges and despise them will be under greater guilt and condemnation. The application is pointed and clear: the Jewish leaders, in rejecting the teaching of Jesus (which, in Matthew's storyline, has been happening more and more), have rejected God's chosen Messiah. They have fallen on the stone (v. 44) and will be crushed as a result.

In the wider context of Matthew's Gospel, this parable is reminding us of the imminent rejection of Jesus by trial and crucifixion, when the prediction of Psalm 118:22 will be fulfilled. According to Matthew, Jesus' hearers realize that the parable has a direct relevance for themselves, and only the high regard in which people hold Jesus prevents them from taking immediate action to arrest him (vv. 45–46).

The parable of the wedding feast (22:1–14)

The story at the centre of this parable is of a wedding given by a king for his son and for which invitations are distributed. Many receive the invitation but make no response. The king sends out many servants, saying that everything is ready. Not only do many refuse to act on the invitation, but also they treat the king's servants shamefully, killing some of them. In anger, the king punishes those who have so mistreated him, and sends the invitation to those who were not originally called.

Although the wedding feast is filled with guests in this way, there is one person present who has no wedding garment on and is therefore not fit to be present. The king has him ejected from the feast.

It seems strange that, having taken such pains to get guests in, the king should then throw one out for what he is wearing! Yet important truths are being taught here. Again, those who have received the blessings of God's covenant salvation—represented by the Jewish religious leaders—are being depicted as those who have despised the grace of their King. Others will receive the gospel instead of them. Yet only with the right preparation can any of us be in the King's presence. Nothing else can secure our salvation but being covered with the wedding garment that satisfies the King.

The King's authority recognized (22:15–46)

Just as the challenge to Jesus' authority is conveyed in three parables, the recognition of that authority is displayed in three short teaching situations in which Jesus is further cast in the role of a prophet. The result of his teaching is that his hearers are astonished, even to the point of being silenced. These teaching sections come about because the religious leaders recognize that the only way to catch Jesus is in his talk (v. 15). The Pharisees are trying to throw hard questions on Jesus and leave him in 'no-win' situations.

First, Jesus gives a pronouncement on paying taxes. With flattery, the religious teachers prepare their ground. Jesus, they know, is not afraid of people, nor of the opinions of others. So does he think it right to pay taxes to Caesar (v. 17)? To answer 'No' could be construed as a challenge to the authority of the emperor; to answer 'Yes' could be seen as a betrayal of his people.

Jesus' answer is brilliant and simple. He asks for a coin on which Caesar's head appears. There are things, says Jesus, that belong to Caesar and must be given to him. There are things that belong to God and must be given to him. In other words, while the Pharisees want to debate what should be given to Caesar, Jesus is highlighting their refusal to give God his due.

Second, the Sadducees, who denied the idea of resurrection, also try to trip up Jesus in his talk. They refer Jesus to the levirate provision of the Old Testament, in which the brother of a dead man was obliged to marry the widow and perpetuate his brother's family line. It is not impossible, the Sadducees argue, for a woman to be married to seven brothers in turn. But in the resurrection, whose wife would she be?

Jesus refuses to stoop to their level. They are ignorant both of the Bible and of the God of the Bible. There are no marriage ties in heaven. Jesus refers to the Old Testament covenant formula in which God describes himself as 'the God of Abraham, and the God of Isaac, and the God of Jacob', and concludes that 'He is not God of the dead, but of the living' (v. 32). Death changes relations on a horizontal level, but not on the vertical level of our relationship to God. Again the answer of Jesus shows his prophetic wisdom and insight. He establishes the authority of the Old Testament, demonstrates the reality of resurrection and silences his accusers.

Third, one of the Sadducees asks Jesus to identify the greatest commandment of the Law. Without hesitation,

Jesus cites Deuteronomy 6:5, part of one of the most important passages of the Old Testament, which demands that we love God with our whole being. He also cites Leviticus 19:18, which requires that we love our neighbour. To Jesus, the whole religion of Scripture is reducible to these two precepts.

This section is closed with a turning of the tables. Jesus puts a question to the Pharisees. It is very simple: Whose son is the Messiah? As experts in the Old Testament, they know the answer: he is the son of David. So Jesus probes further: How then can David call the Messiah his Lord? He cites Psalm 110:1 to illustrate the question. In that psalm, David calls the person whom the Lord Jehovah exalts to his right hand his Lord and Master. The psalm is clearly messianic, but the religious experts have difficulty reconciling Davidic sonship with the lordship of which the psalm speaks.

Matthew's use of this passage is not simply as a convenient way to round off the question-and-answer session which demonstrates the King's authority; it is also at the heart of the theme of his Gospel. Jesus is the Messiah, the son of David. That fact is established in the opening verses of the Gospel. But the psalmist anticipates the elevation of David's son to the highest place in God's presence. Matthew is anticipating the closing movements of his Gospel, as David's son and Lord is rejected prior to his exaltation to glory.

The King's authority in cursing his enemies (23:1–39)

The seven woes of Matthew 23 serve as a direct response to the Pharisees and Sadducees who have been questioning him, trying to trap and entangle him in his teaching. Many of these woes address directly the pretence of these religious leaders that they are teachers of others; they are themselves in need of teaching.

But the woes also stand as a contrast with the beatitudes of chapter 5. There the King's blessing was pronounced on his people in a series of nine benedictions which contrast markedly with the series of maledictions, or curses, of this chapter. It is a solemn chapter, one in which the King's curse upon his enemies is coupled with his lament over the situation that leads to such a response.

But the woes also stand as a contrast with the beatitudes of chapter 5. There the King's blessing was pronounced on his people in a series of nine benedictions which contrast markedly with the series of maledictions, or curses, of this chapter.

Why does he pronounce these woes on the 'scribes and Pharisees' (v. 2)? Because of their hypocrisy. This is an important concept in Matthew's Gospel, with words relating to 'hypocrisy' appearing some fourteen times in the course of the book. Half of these occurrences are in this chapter. The word 'hypocrite' comes from the Greek word for an actor's mask. In the Greek theatre, there were two types of play—the comedy and the tragedy. In a comedy, the actor would wear a mask with a huge smile; in a tragedy, with a huge frown or a sad face. Whatever the mask, it represented the actor in character, not the real person.

In religion too, according to Jesus, we can play a part. Our religious observance can mask what we truly are. This chapter teaches us some of the characteristics of hypocrisy in religion. It also tells us where hypocrisy comes from—from preaching one thing but not practising it (see v. 3). The religious leaders of Jesus' day were good at placing religious duties like burdens on the shoulders of people, parading their religion before others, and being greeted and entitled 'rabbi'. In short, they were self-exalting people who never applied to themselves the strictures they placed on the lives of others. Jesus warns that such behaviour will lead to ruin, because God exalts the humble and humbles the proud (v. 12).

What, then, are hypocrites like?

- They shut people out of the kingdom of God by their own example and teaching (v. 13).
- They travel the world to get a convert and then make him a child of hell (v. 15).
- They change their rules to suit themselves, qualifying the requirements of God's law to allow latitude in some areas but not in others (vv. 16–21).
- They make minor things important while leaving major things undone (vv. 23–24).
- They are concerned with external purity while inside they are unclean (vv. 25–26).
- They appear to be morally upright before men, even though they are full of lawlessness (vv. 27–28).
- They boast in the past while failing to live according to the example of faith from the past (vv. 29–32).

Such behaviour can never please God. Jesus tells his hearers that there is nothing new in all of this: since Abel was murdered at the beginning of human history, right down to the murder of

Zechariah in the temple, God's true followers have been persecuted by those who profess to be the true church. A day of reckoning is coming, however. God will not be mocked.

The prophetic ministry of Jesus, therefore, includes the authority to speak in judgement over others. As Alistair Wilson says, 'In pronouncing these woes, Jesus was not merely attacking verbally those who did not agree with him but he was formally pronouncing judgement on the Jewish leaders in a way that implies that he had the authority to do such a thing.'[3]

Therefore, both the actions—of riding into Jerusalem, cleansing the temple and cursing the fig tree—and the teaching of these chapters portray Jesus as the King whose words are authoritative and true.

None of this, however, is uttered as a cold, heartless diatribe. In fact, Jesus bewails this behaviour in the deepest sense. He laments over Jerusalem (v. 37), which knew so many privileges and enjoyed so many blessings, and which responded by killing the messengers of God, just as the parable of the tenants (21:33–41) illustrated.

It was not for any reason in God that Jerusalem did not enjoy the blessing of God's covenant salvation. In Jesus Christ, God had come down to Jerusalem; David's son, the messianic King, had come into Jerusalem. Jesus telescopes his point of reference; what God has been doing down through the ages, Jesus has been doing over the past three years: pleading with Jerusalem to repent. Instead, Jerusalem is now on the brink of shedding innocent blood again, this time by rejecting Jesus himself.

For further study ▶

FOR FURTHER STUDY

1. Compare 21:13 with Isaiah 56:7 and Jeremiah 7:11. What do these passages tell us about the use of our places of worship?
2. Among New Testament places, Bethany (21:17) is important to Jesus. Read the following passages: John 11:1–44; John 12:1–8; Luke 24:50. What events took place at Bethany?
3. Who do the two sons in the parable of 21:28–32 represent?
4. Jesus quotes from Psalm 118 in 21:42. How does he interpret the verse he quotes? How is the same verse used in Acts 4:11 and 1 Peter 2:7?
5. How is the formula 'the God of Abraham, and the God of Isaac, and the God of Jacob' (22:32) related to belief in the resurrection?

TO THINK ABOUT AND DISCUSS

1. In what ways can we turn the church of Christ into a 'den of robbers'?
2. Do you think Jesus is guaranteeing the success of all our prayers in 21:22? If we do not get what we ask for, is it because we do not have enough faith?
3. How do we distribute the wedding invitation to the gospel banquet (22:9)?
4. Chapter 23 combines Jesus' severe judgement on hypocrites with his sincere lament over Jerusalem. How can we ensure we strike the right balance between boldness in declaring the truth of God's judgement and warmth towards those who deserve it? How can we prevent boldness from becoming coldness?

12 The King is coming again

(24:1–25:46)

In the Old Testament, God's messengers spoke out God's message. Often, that included predicting the future. Jesus' prophetic ministry contains a strong element of prediction, not least in this section of the Gospel.

The last block of teaching in Matthew's Gospel concerns the end of the age; it is eschatological in focus. Its importance is seen in the fact that all three Synoptic Gospels have a version of this teaching (see Mark 13 and Luke 21). It is often referred to as the Olivet discourse, since it was delivered on the Mount of Olives (24:3).

The King's authority in predicting the future (24:1–51)

Several observations are in order regarding this section.

First, the Olivet discourse is prompted by the prospect of the destruction of the temple (vv. 1–2). Its buildings appear so inviolable and indestructible, yet Jesus makes the claim, not merely that the temple *might* be destroyed, but that it *will* be destroyed, stone by stone.

Second, the discourse is in response to the disciples' enquiry on three fundamentally important issues. They ask three questions: When will these things be? What will be the sign of Jesus' coming? What will be the sign of the close of the age? Jesus takes up these issues in this chapter. He speaks of times and signs, speaking with authority (one of Matthew's great themes) on the issues of the end times.

Third, the discourse again reveals Jesus as Prophet, predicting the future. He is not just analysing contemporary culture or suggesting methods of discipleship; he is setting himself apart from those who would deceive and lead astray, and he calls for our complete allegiance to his words and predictions.

Fourth, the discourse has a twofold focus, as much Old Testament prophecy does. When Nathan, for example, prophesies in 2 Samuel 7:12 that David's offspring will sit on his throne, the prophecy has an immediate reference to Solomon, but an ultimate reference to Jesus Christ, the greater Son of David. Similarly here: the predictions of this 'little apocalypse', as the chapter is sometimes called, focus, in the first instance, on the destruction of Jerusalem in AD 70, but have an ultimate fulfilment in the end of the world. So when Jesus talks of the impact of a calamity so great that people flee to the mountains, and expresses sorrow for those who will be pregnant and nursing infants in the days of the tribulation, he is focusing first on the fall of Jerusalem, which then becomes a symbol of the destruction of the world as we know it. There is one meaning to Jesus' words, but there are many applications of it.

Fifth, the discourse sets before us the fact that the second coming of Jesus and the end of the world will occur together. They are simultaneous events. The present order will run until Jesus comes again. When he comes, he will close the final chapter in the history of the world. The disciples ask regarding the sign of Jesus' coming, which is referred to in verse 30; then the Son of Man will be revealed in power. This coming will be a terror to unbelievers but a great comfort to Christians: 'The parable of the fig tree [vv. 32–33] is given simply for the purpose of illustrating and enforcing the expectancy and rejoicing that the events, so terrifying to unbelievers, should evoke in believers.'[1]

This passage—like its equivalent in Mark 13—has caused much discussion, particularly in attempts to integrate it into the wider teaching of the Bible regarding the future. However, we can approach the passage by highlighting four key texts that set before us four points along which we can trace Jesus' teaching about the last days.

Point 1: This must take place, but the end is not yet (vv. 3–14)

Jesus makes it clear that there are things that will happen in the world before his return. These include 'wars and rumours of wars … famines and earthquakes in various places' (vv. 6–7). These are dislocations in the natural order which Jesus compares to 'birth pains' (v. 8; compare Rom. 8:22). It is interesting that the comparison is to the pains of a woman giving birth, not to the pains of someone dying. These are birth pangs, not death pangs, and will result in something glorious.

However, the natural disasters will be accompanied by spiritual declension. The church will experience persecution, with apparent Christians betraying other Christians and turning away from their profession of faith. The sign of genuine Christianity, according to Jesus, is not that people start living a life of discipleship, but that they complete it! It is those who 'endure to the end' who will be saved (v. 13). In spite of these difficulties, however, the gospel will continue to be preached.

The natural disasters will be accompanied by spiritual declension. The church will experience persecution, with apparent Christians betraying other Christians and turning away from their profession of faith.

This state of affairs should not lead to pessimism, however. Some readers of the Bible have focused on passages like this and have suggested that we can expect nothing in the days preceding our Lord's return but gradual spiritual decline. The fact that the gospel is to be preached is, however, an indication that the decline in some places will be matched by growth and blessing in others, since the Word of God always results in sinners being saved. We must, therefore, persevere with the worldwide evangelization of the nations, knowing that Jesus will return.

Point 2: For the sake of the elect these days will be cut short (vv. 15–28)

In addition to a state of affairs in which the general principles of the first part of the chapter will be fulfilled, Jesus reminds us that there are events that will take place to fulfil specific prophecy before Jesus comes. Jesus refers generally to the prophecy of Daniel, but seems specifically to be referring to the following predictions:

- Daniel 9:27: '… on the wing of abominations shall come one who makes desolate, until the decreed end is poured out on the desolator.'
- Daniel 11:31–2: '… they shall set up the abomination that makes desolate. He shall seduce with flattery those who violate the covenant, but the people who know their God shall stand firm and take action.'
- Daniel 12:11: '… from the time that the regular burnt offering is taken away and the abomination that makes desolate is set up, there shall be 1,290 days.'

Daniel's prediction seems to have been fulfilled when Antiochus Epiphanes erected an altar to the Greek god Zeus in the temple and offered a pig on it in 168 BC. This was a direct affront to the people of God. But the prediction telescopes, and Jesus uses this prophecy to speak of the Roman armies assaulting Jerusalem. Just as God was affronted then, so he will be affronted again. For the loyal people of God this will be the beginning of a long period of persecution, during which many Christians will be killed and will have to flee from Jerusalem. Holy places and holy times (note the reference to the Sabbath in v. 20) will be desecrated. This will be the beginning of tribulation on an unprecedented scale.

This is not a different set of circumstances from that described in verses 9–14, but a recapitulation of the prophecy in the light of the Old Testament. Daniel's prophecy is to be fulfilled several times over.

The subtlety of Satan is seen in the fact that false prophets will appear, promising to give an easier option and to be the true prophets of God. So the church will be physically persecuted but will also be tempted to embrace seductive and attractive heresies. These have always been Satan's twin weapons against the church.

However, God will not leave his people in this situation for ever. For the sake of his own people he will shorten the days of trial. His appearance will be as sudden as a flash of lightning, and the trials and tribulations of his people will come to an end (v. 27).

Point 3: They will see the Son of Man coming in the clouds of heaven (vv. 29–41)

The trials and tribulations of the church in the world will be brought to an end with the return of Jesus Christ. His return will be unmistakeable, and there are things that will happen only when Jesus comes.

Jesus uses an illustration from nature to describe his return. Just as a tree changes with the changing seasons, so the events and situations he has described will herald his return. His word is certain and will not pass away, unlike the created universe.

Jesus reminds us that we do not know when he is coming again. This does not contradict the earlier teaching of the chapter, that certain events must first take place. Only God knows the time of the end of the world. Indeed, in a remarkable statement which reminds us that Jesus is the Servant of God while he is in the world, he reminds us that even he does not know the time of his own return; that belongs to the Father, whose Servant he is (v. 36).

When Jesus returns, it will be like Noah's flood, which

had been predicted; however, people ignored the prediction until it was too late. The second coming of Jesus will break into the ordinary activities of life and will cause disruption and division.

One point of difficulty over this passage is Jesus' prediction that these events will take place within the current generation (v. 34). If we see him running the destruction of Jerusalem together with his own return in prophetic prediction, we will understand his meaning. The destruction of Jerusalem would take place before many of his hearers died; but the same pattern of sudden, swift, merciless judgement will accompany his return at the end of time.

Point 4: You must also be ready (vv. 42–51)

In the light of all this, there are things to which we must attend before Jesus comes, so that we will be ready for it. Just as a wise house-owner guards against the theft of his or her property, so we must be ready for the coming of the Son of Man, which will take us by surprise.

Just as servants are left to look after a property in the absence of a master, so we, too, have been left to live wisely and well while Jesus is absent. But one day, Jesus, our Master, will return to review his servants and their work. That day will be unexpected, and the only way to prepare for it is to say, 'It may be today—let's make sure we are working, and that we are ready!'

The King's authority in final judgement (25:1–46)

The theme of judgement is prominent in the three parts of this chapter.

Jesus' parable of the ten virgins (vv. 1–13) continues his teaching on the end of the world and the coming of the Son of Man for judgement. But it also links to all that he has previously taught about his work and mission. In chapter 13, for example, the parables begin with the words 'the kingdom of heaven is like ...' and highlight aspects of the teaching of Jesus regarding the kingdom that are relevant for us in the present. Now, however, Jesus begins with the words '*Then* the kingdom of heaven will be like ...' (25:1, emphasis added). The existence of the kingdom of heaven continues across time, history and space. It has broken into our history through the incarnation of Jesus; and what he did will continue to have an effect on the lives of individuals to the end.

Once again, Matthew records a parable with a wedding theme. The 'virgins' are those who, like modern bridesmaids, accompany the bride; in the custom of Jesus' day they would accompany her to the bridegroom's house. This is one of several parables in Matthew which draw on wedding imagery.

In this particular parable, half of the maidens are wise enough to make preparation for the arrival of the bridegroom, whenever that may be; the other five make no preparation. When the bridegroom's arrival is delayed, the women become sleepy, so that the midnight cry heralding his appearance takes them all by surprise. Those who are prepared, with plenty of oil in their lamps, are ready to meet the bridegroom, while those who have not made preparation are caught unawares.

The main point of the parable is the surprise element of the coming of the bridegroom. Jesus drives that point home in the advice of verse 13: 'Watch therefore, for you know neither the day nor the hour.' Jesus is going to come again, and when he does the true nature of the kingdom of heaven will be manifested; those who followed and served him in the world will be ready to meet him when he comes again.

The parable of the talents (vv. 14–30) is also part of the teaching of Jesus regarding the second coming and is designed to encourage us to be faithful to Christ until he comes again.

The 'talents' in the parable are items of money, and the story is of an absent master who gives various sums of money to his servants. Two of them are faithful and one is not. The one who is not is punished for his laziness.

This servant's complaint is that the master is 'hard' and expected too much; perhaps he is also complaining that the master was away and doing business in foreign lands instead of remaining at home.

This is a lie, of course; it is the master's right to give the money to whomever he wishes, and to demand what he wishes. The lie is an excuse to cover the servant's own lack of industry.

The talent is given to the one who has ten, proving the point of Matthew 13:12, that 'to the one who has, more will be given, and he will have an abundance, but from the one who has not, even what he has will be taken away'.

It is not necessary for us to find a spiritual meaning in every detail of the story. But the context shows us that its meaning is that, if we fail to use our possessions, gifts and time for the Lord while he is away from us in heaven, then we will lose everything when he comes again.

The final part of the chapter is concerned with the final judgement (vv. 31–46). Although it is told using illustrative language, with the final judgement being compared to a shepherd separating sheep from goats, it is not a parable. It reads almost like an exact description of what will happen when Jesus comes again, as if Jesus wants to make explicit what was implicit in the parables.

This is a very moving and very solemn passage. It reminds us of certain things that will be true about the return of the Lord Jesus Christ.

He will come in glory (v. 31)

There is the greatest contrast drawn between the first appearance of Jesus and the second one. Whereas his first appearance was in obscurity, his second will be in glory. The references to the presence of the angels and the glorious throne further emphasize the fact that this second coming will be a revelation of the greatest glory imaginable.

He will separate the nations (vv. 32–33)

It is interesting that, just when Jesus is about to be judged by the people, he declares that a day is coming when he will judge the people. He compares himself to a shepherd who separates his sheep from goats. This concept has an important Old Testament background (see, for example, the references to judgement in Isaiah 11:3–4 and to the shepherd in Ezekiel 34:17[2]). Although we may classify people in many different ways, the important distinctions are those set by God himself and applied by Jesus in final judgement.

He will bring his people into the presence of God (vv. 34–40)

His people are those who have served him and whose service

has been evident in a life of devotion to him. Matthew is not telling us that people who do good things will go to heaven; rather, he is telling us that good things are an evidence of true discipleship and genuine faith. Those who are saved by faith are judged by their works, since their works show how much they were willing to deny themselves in the service of others. The phrase 'you did it to me' (v. 40) is a clear indicator of the Christ-centred and Christlike character of their religion. The faith that saves by trusting to the work of Christ shows itself to be genuine by its fruits and practical consequences. Those who have served Christ in this way enjoy the inheritance prepared for them; they enter into the final reality of the kingdom of heaven.

He will banish the wicked into eternal fire (vv. 41–46)

In a similar way, those who have lived their lives without any reference to God have demonstrated this by their self-centredness and self-interest. There were no deeds of kindness, nothing at all done out of love to God. These do not inherit a kingdom prepared for them, but one which was prepared for the devil and his angels. This is one of the clearest evidences in the New Testament that there is a dark side to the good news of the gospel: those who believe in Jesus will go with him to heaven, but those who do not will reap the consequences of what they have sown in eternal punishment.

The King is the final Judge; he will deal in strict justice with us all and will not be mocked in his ultimate review of the nations.

For further study ▶

FOR FURTHER STUDY

1. According to 24:6–7, what events will precede Jesus' return? How do you see this being fulfilled today?
2. The New Testament warns about false prophets. What do the following passages teach on this subject: Acts 20:29; 2 Corinthians 11:1–6; Galatians 1:6–9; 2 Thessalonians 2:3–4; Jude 3–4?
3. How is the 'trumpet call' of 24:31 to be understood? Compare this verse with 1 Corinthians 15:52 and 1 Thessalonians 4:16.
4. What are the three scenes of Matthew 25? What point are they making? What are the points of similarity and contrast between them?

TO THINK ABOUT AND DISCUSS

1. Is it right for Christians to speculate about the last things?
2. In the light of 24:9–12, should we be optimistic or pessimistic about the future?
3. How can we decide whether or not someone is a false prophet?
4. Does hell exist? How can we believe in the reality of hell? What is suggested in 24:51 and 25:45–46 about the nature of hell?

13 The King dies

(26:1–27:66)

The dark events that lead to the cross are central to Matthew's purpose. It is in Christ's dying that we see the greatness of God's King. This is how he is going to destroy death itself and save his people from their sins.

Matthew devotes two chapters to the passion and suffering of Jesus. These last hours of his life are emphasized more than any other period of his ministry. The Gospels are not biographies: they were written for very clear purposes, which is why more attention was given to the last three years of his life than to the previous thirty, and proportionally more to the last week of his life than to the rest of his public ministry. The cross is dominant, and the record of Jesus' journey to the cross is one of the most moving records in all of literature.

We can look at Jesus' death in terms of several relationships that develop in the course of the narrative.

Jesus and his enemies (26:1–5)

The formula 'When Jesus had finished all these sayings' appears again at 26:1, signifying that we move from the block of teaching to the narrative. Jesus predicts his death once again (see, for example 17:22–23), only now it is imminent. 'Passover is coming,' he says; this is the memorial feast for the Jewish people, the time when they look back at the redemption from Egypt through the death of the Passover lamb. Now Jesus is going to fulfil that typology and die for the salvation of his people.

As Jesus informs the disciples of his approaching death, the chief priests and popular leaders are plotting to arrest Jesus. They want him dead, and only the timing of the religious festival prevents them from carrying out the plot.

Yet, as Matthew weaves these aspects together, we are conscious, on the one hand, of the hypocrisy of these enemies of the King, but also, on the other hand, of the way in which God works out his sovereign purposes. The religious leaders will not murder Jesus now, for religious reasons; yet they do not reflect on the sinfulness of their design and plan! Murder is not justified at any time. Their plans show the warped nature of their thinking.

But Jesus gives us a glimpse here of the way in which God is working out his purposes. The Son of Man *will* be delivered—this is something God has ordained from all eternity. The plans being hatched in secret cannot be excused, yet they are the means by which God's sovereign will is to be executed. Even the wrath of man will praise God (Ps. 76:10).

Jesus and the woman (26:6–13)

At this point, Jesus is at Bethany, reclining for supper in the house of Simon. There he is anointed by a woman who empties an expensive jar of oil onto his head. The disciples are angry because of the wastefulness of the action. Yet Jesus defends her, stating that the anointing is, in fact, a preparation for burial, and that her action will always be commemorated wherever the gospel is preached.

There is a slight problem here over the relationship of this anointing (also recounted in Mark 14:3–9) to those of the sinful woman in Luke 7:36–50 and Mary in John 12:1–8. Who anointed Jesus in Matthew 26, and was this something that happened twice in his life, earlier (as Luke suggests) and later (as Matthew suggests)? Or was there just one anointing?

It would appear that Jesus was, indeed, anointed twice, and that Mary was the woman who anointed Jesus in Matthew 26, as an act of love for Jesus as he was about to be crucified. Jesus' statement that this is a suitable act before burial is important, since women will come to anoint the body of Jesus (Luke 24:1) but will be unable to do so. This is the time for Mary to act, and she does so willingly. Jesus' rebuke to the disciples is also important, since they have failed to grasp this opportunity which Mary takes to show her devotion to Jesus.

We should not lose sight of the echo here of the anointing with the Holy Spirit that took place in chapter 3. Jesus was anointed by God in preparation for his public ministry; he is now anointed by the woman in preparation for his death and burial. The first anointing was in preparation for the work of his life; the second is in preparation for the work of his death.

Jesus and the disciples (26:14–35)

Matthew deliberately draws our attention to the contrast between Judas and the rest of the disciples. Judas is scheming with the religious leaders and he strikes a deal with them to hand Jesus over to them for thirty pieces of silver.

When Jesus sits down with his disciples to keep the Passover, he demonstrates his awareness of what Judas is about by identifying him as the one who will betray him. The righteousness of Jesus is contrasted with the sin of Judas. Jesus obeys the will of God, not only by keeping the Passover meal, but also by identifying himself as being under necessity to die: 'The Son of Man goes as it is written of him' (v. 24). Judas, on the other hand, is under the curse of God: Jesus pronounces a woe upon him (v. 24), just as he had on the unrepentant cities of the district.

At some point in the meal, Judas leaves and the other disciples receive the blessing of a new covenant meal, in which the Passover is transformed into the Lord's Supper. The breaking and eating of unleavened bread was part of the Passover ritual; so, too, was the drinking of wine. Four cups of wine would have been taken, and during each a portion of Exodus 6 would have been read. The various elements of the meal would also have included the singing of parts of Psalms 113–118. The mention in verse 30 of the singing of a song of praise is important.

While the bread is being distributed, Jesus imparts new significance to it, making it symbolic of his own body. Each time they break bread they will think about his death on the cross. Similarly, Jesus gives new meaning to the wine, which he describes as 'my blood of the covenant, which is poured out for many for the forgiveness of sins' (v. 28). These words cast us back into the Old Testament, with its many references to blood poured out in sacrifice and sprinkled on the people for their forgiveness and consecration (see, for example, Exod. 24:8).

Some have interpreted Jesus' words literally and have developed the view that the bread and wine actually become the body and blood of Christ. But neither Scripture nor reason supports that view. It is better to understand Jesus' words to mean that these elements serve both as a memorial, so that we will look back to the work of Christ on the cross, and as a means of grace, by which, through faith, we feed on Christ spiritually.

There is also a forward-looking, prospective dimension to the Lord's Supper, as Jesus anticipates a heavenly banquet with his people in his Father's kingdom (v. 29).

A dark note is introduced after they leave the upper room and go out to the Mount of Olives. Jesus tells them of the fulfilment of another Old Testament prophecy: just as Zechariah 13:7 indicated, the flock of Christ will be scattered with the smiting of the shepherd. The meaning is that the disciples will 'fall away' (v. 31); they will be offended by Christ and will distance themselves from him.

Peter refuses to believe that he is capable of such action and he denies that he will be offended. Jesus predicts that, before the night is out, Peter will deny knowing Jesus, not once, but three times.

The air is obviously heavy; Judas will betray Jesus, all will be offended by Jesus and Peter will deny Jesus. The new Supper Jesus has given his followers, the new kingdom meal, is itself heavy with the coming storm of his death on the cross. Yet Jesus is not going to die a martyr's death; his speech is laced with the greatest faith, assurance and hope. The Supper anticipates a glorious future and, in the nearer future, Jesus knows that he will be raised up and will be in Galilee before them (v. 32). Jesus loses no confidence as he approaches his end. He goes to his cross as a man of great faith.

Jesus and his Father (26:36–46)

Jesus' experience in Gethsemane is a solemn and powerful time when he wrestles with his Father in prayer in connection with his coming death. He commissions Peter, James and John to accompany him and to 'watch' with him (v. 38). It is surely an indication of his great humiliation that he relies in this moment on the presence of three disciples for strengthening and encouragement. Yet they are not equal to the task, and fall asleep.

Professor Roderick Finlayson introduces the passage to us:

> His destination was the Garden, a place to which he had frequently resorted for communion and refreshment. But this time it was to be the place of conflict, the place where he should have not only a preview, but a foretaste of the cross. This was something more intimate, more distressing, than he had hitherto experienced. And in approaching this solemn study, we must tread reverently and cautiously.

> Gethsemane is not a field for intellect, it is a sanctuary for faith. There was transacted something that brings us completely out of our depth, yet something that has such a distinct bearing on our redemption that we dare not pass it by.[1]

Matthew highlights three things for us in his account of Jesus' foretaste of the cross in the garden of Gethsemane.

The depth of Jesus' sorrow (vv. 37–38)

Matthew tells us that Jesus 'began to be *sorrowful* and *troubled*'. Jesus says to the disciples that his soul is '*very sorrowful*, even to death' (emphasis added). These words are indicators of deep emotional distress. The emotional life of Jesus makes a fascinating study, and here the inner life of Jesus' soul is before our view. He is shaken to the core of his being. He has descended into earth's lower parts from his heights of glory, yet still more suffering awaits him. As B. B. Warfield puts it, 'In these supreme moments, our Lord sounded the ultimate depths of human anguish, and vindicated on the score of the intensity of his mental sufferings the right to the title of Man of Sorrows.'[2]

The intensity of Jesus' prayer (vv. 39–44)

The subject of Jesus' prayer is the cup which the Father is giving him to drink. He shared a cup with his disciples, which all of them are to drink as a memorial to him; but his cup is unique and can be shared by none other. It represents all that Calvary will be in his experience; it consists 'in the imputation to him of a criminal's guilt, and the assignment to him of a criminal's position and destiny'.[3]

It is a cup from which Jesus naturally recoils, praying to

his Father that, if it is possible, the cup should pass him by. Three times he prays in this way, with the same words, not because he wants to avoid the Father's will for him but precisely because he does not. Only in prayer can Jesus prepare himself adequately for the conflict before him; by praying in this way and at this time, Jesus leaves his followers a great example.

The strength of Jesus' resolve (vv. 39,45–46)

Matthew reminds us that Jesus' prayers not only sound the note of the possibility of a different portion for him; they also express his complete resignation to the Father's will: 'not as I will, but as you will' (v. 39). It is in wrestling with God in this way that Jesus is able to rouse his sleeping disciples and lead them into the conflict with those who have come to claim the Son of Man (v. 46).

Jesus and his accusers (26:47–68)

Matthew's account of the arrest of Jesus follows a clear sequence. First, Jesus is handed over in the garden of Gethsemane by Judas, who leads a large crowd of people, kisses Jesus and thereby marks him out as the one they want. One of the disciples (Matthew doesn't tell us who, but we know from John 18:10 that it is Peter) tries to defend Jesus by force, strikes out at the servant of the high priest and only wounds him on the side of his head. Jesus heals him (according to Luke 22:51) and, with a quiet dignity, places himself in the hands of his captors, knowing that these events are fulfilling the Scriptures. True also to his prediction, all the disciples flee the scene.

The drama now shifts to the courtyard of Caiaphas the high priest, one of the leading religious figures among the Jews. There is both a religious and a civil trial; church and state are united in their rejection of God's true messianic King.

The integrity and probity of Jesus are highlighted by the fact that any accusation against him can only be made by false testimony delivered by false witnesses. He is accused of plotting the destruction of the temple, but he remains silent.

The high priest then demands that he answer the charge that he claims to be the Son of God. Jesus' answer that he will one day be seen coming in the clouds and with great glory leads to the charge of blasphemy against him. At first glance, it is difficult to see where the blasphemy lies, but Darrell Bock suggests that the attack on the Jewish leadership is enough to count for a charge of blasphemy:

> [Jesus] attacked the leadership, by implicitly claiming to be their future judge ... This would be seen as a violation of Exodus 22:28, where God's leaders are not to be cursed. A claim that their authority was non-existent and that they would be accounted among the wicked is a total rejection of their authority. To the leadership, this was an affront to God as they were, in their own view, God's established chosen leadership.[4]

The religious leaders therefore unite in their conclusion: 'He deserves death' (v. 66).

Jesus and Peter (26:69–75)

All this time, Peter has been keeping a safe distance out in the courtyard. A servant girl recognizes him as having been among Jesus' followers. Peter strenuously denies this. As Peter moves away, another girl also recognizes him. Again he denies knowing Jesus of Nazareth. A third similar statement evokes not only a denial, but also cursing and swearing. Peter is not conscious of fulfilling Jesus' prediction until the cock crows and brings it all home—his bravado, his claim to remain loyal when everyone else deserts Jesus, his self-confidence. Peter is reduced to bitter tears as he recalls the saying of Jesus. Luke (22:61) adds the detail that Jesus turns to look at Peter, a look both of love and of sorrow that must pierce Peter's heart.

Jesus and Pilate (27:1–26)

The trial now moves from ecclesiastical courts to civil courts and Jesus is led before the Roman governor, Pilate. Palestine had been under the authority and domination of Rome since 63 BC, when Pompey took it over and made it a province of Syria. Palestine had proved to be a turbulent province, so Rome stationed a procurator (or 'governor', 27:11) in Palestine who was directly answerable to the emperor. At the time of Jesus' death, the Roman emperor was Tiberius and the governor was the procurator Pontius Pilate, who remained in that post from AD 26 to 36.

There was always an uneasy peace between the Jewish leaders and the Roman authorities. Luke, however, supplies the interesting detail that the trial of Jesus brokered a strange union between them: 'Herod and Pilate became friends with each other that very day, for before this they had been at enmity with each other' (Luke 23:12).

As Ann Wroe points out in her study of Pilate, 'He did not

judge all cases: the Jews had been left with considerable autonomy. But he had the power of review, and in general the more serious the charge, the more likely he was to handle it. This was true even in religious cases.'[5] So it was that, in order to succeed in their death charge, the Jewish leaders presented Jesus to Pilate.

In the meantime, Judas is filled with remorse for his deeds. The money he has gained for betraying Jesus is burning a hole in his very soul. Protesting the innocence of Jesus, he tries to return it, but the religious leaders will not accept it. In a fit of darkness, Judas takes his own life and his money is used to buy a piece of ground where he is subsequently buried. It is called the Field of Blood (v. 8); in these events, Matthew sees a fulfilment of Zechariah 11:13. Matthew 27:9 attributes the prophecy to Jeremiah, probably because the events reflect both the Zechariah allusion of thirty pieces of silver being thrown down in the house of the Lord and the references in Jeremiah 19 to the shedding of innocent blood and the breaking of the potter's flask. Matthew is not seeing here simply the fulfilment of individual prophecies, but rather the development of 'Old Testament patterns' of apostasy and rejection which have now culminated in the events around the trial of Jesus.[6]

Judas is filled with remorse for his deeds. The money he has gained for betraying Jesus is burning a hole in his very soul.

The trial before Pilate now advances in three stages:

First, Pilate interviews Jesus, asking him directly if he claims to be 'King of the Jews'. Amid the clamour of the religious leaders, Jesus remains silent. This surprises Pilate; no prisoner has ever acted in this way before.

Second, Pilate offers to release Jesus according to a local custom at the time of religious festivities. Pilate knows that Barabbas, 'a notorious prisoner' (v. 16), is awaiting crucifixion, and he gambles on the crowd releasing Jesus. Pilate is also motivated by a message from his wife, Procula, protesting the innocence of Jesus on the basis of a dream about him that has troubled her. It seems a superstitious element in the story, and Matthew alone records it, but it is also highly realistic and there is no reason to think that Pilate was unaffected by it.

Indeed, it is a main reason for Pilate delaying a verdict and continuing to play with the will of the crowd. He ends up offering the crowd a choice: 'Which of the two do you want me to release for you?' he asks. Ann Wroe comments: 'By asking the question, "Jesus or Barabbas?" he had already rejected the claims of Jesus. By placing the two on the same level, two criminals who could be taken or left, he had already ranged himself with Christ's enemies.'[7] The crowd shouts, 'Let him be crucified!' (v. 22).

Third, Pilate delivers the verdict. It is a tense moment, and the feelings of the crowd are growing stronger and more agitated. Pilate has had enough; he hands the prisoner over to the crowd, which responds by taking responsibility for his blood. Pilate orders that Jesus be whipped. The die has been cast.

Jesus and his cross (27:27–56)

The humiliation of Jesus continues. First he is parodied, as the crowd dress him in a mock robe and crown. The crown is made of thorns that dig into his head. They ridicule him and cry, 'Hail, King of the Jews!'

They then lead him away for crucifixion. This involves Jesus carrying the cross-beam of his own cross to the place of execution. Simon, a Cyrenian, is compelled to assist him. The site of the crucifixion is called 'Golgotha', and the details are stark. Matthew draws our attention to the following elements of the drama, most of which fulfil Old Testament predictions:

- They offer him a mixture of wine and vinegar (compare Ps. 69:21).
- They gamble for his clothes (compare Ps. 22:18).
- They place the words 'King of the Jews' over his head.
- They crucify him between two thieves (compare Isa. 53:12).
- They mock his claim to be able to rebuild the temple after three days, when he cannot save himself.
- They unwittingly cite Psalm 22:8—'He trusts in God; let God deliver him now.'

The death of Jesus takes place in darkness. Darkness engulfs the world for three hours, from noon until 3 p.m. (v. 45). He hangs on the cross for six hours. Crucifixion was a notoriously painful death; the Latin word for a cross is at the root of both the word 'crucify' and the word 'excruciating'. Not only was there physical torture involved, but death was caused by drowning, as the person crucified was eventually unable to raise his or her body sufficiently to take a breath, so that the lungs filled with moisture. For the first three hours of his pain, Jesus hangs in view of the world that has rejected him. For the next three hours, he is in darkness.

In the opening scenes of Matthew's Gospel, Jesus' birth is marked by a supernatural light (at midnight?) that guides wise men to the manger (2:2); in an interesting contrast, his death is marked by a supernatural darkness at noon that accentuates the loneliness of the Christ on the cross.

Together the Gospels record seven sayings of Jesus on the cross, but Matthew records only one of them, the sixth: 'My God, my God, why have you forsaken me' (v. 46). That Jesus should refer to his Father as his God is interesting. He is recorded as doing this on only one other occasion (John 20:17). Clearly, on the cross, his covenant relationship to God is to the fore. He is speaking as the messianic King who is also the messianic Servant of God (see Isa. 42:1).

The Aramaic expression for 'my God' is similar to the name of Elijah, so, once again in Matthew's Gospel, there is a reference to Elijah, as the bystanders mistakenly think that Jesus is calling on Elijah to rescue him (v. 47). But there is no rescue; just one final cry and one final breath.

Matthew draws our attention, however, to various phenomena that occur at the moment of Jesus' death. First, the curtain of the temple is torn in two (v. 51). This is the veil that separated the Most Holy Place from the rest of the temple structure (see, for example, the description in 2 Chr. 3:14). It was a heavily embroidered curtain, one not easily torn; further, the tear is from top to bottom, symbolizing that the hands of heaven are responsible for the splitting of it into two. Again we need to pick up a contrast with earlier themes, particularly the opening of the heavens at the baptism of Jesus (3:16), which the tearing of the veil echoes, since it symbolizes that a way into the presence of God has now been made possible.

Second, an earthquake occurs (v. 51). The fact that the Creator of the earth has died is enough to convulse the physical universe. A star in the sky heralded his birth; a shaking of the earth heralds his death. The world itself shakes as the body and spirit of its Maker are separated from each other.

Third, graves open, and many dead saints are revived (v. 52). This must have caused great astonishment to those who saw them appear from their tombs. Yet the fact that they did so was itself an evidence of the fact that the King had entered the territory of his enemy to defeat him on his own ground.

Fourth, the centurion bears testimony to the deity of Jesus with his confession, amid these remarkable scenes, that this is truly the Son of God (v. 54). Once again in Matthew's Gospel, it is left to a Gentile to express great faith when the disciples have fled the scene.

Not all the followers of Jesus have left, of course. There are the women; and Matthew recounts the names of those who are last at the cross and who will also be first at the grave: Mary Magdalene, Jesus' own mother, and the wife of Zebedee (v. 56).

Jesus and his friends (27:57–66)

One other remarkable act of loyalty takes place at this moment, as Joseph, a wealthy man from Arimathea, steps forward and asks that he might have Jesus' body. He makes arrangements for it to be buried in a new tomb, over the entrance of which he carefully places a large stone. The women keep vigil close by (v. 61). Thus Jesus, having fulfilled the part of Isaiah's prophecy that said he would be numbered with sinners (Isa. 53:12), fulfils another part of the same prophecy: the prediction of an association in death with a rich man (Isa. 53:9).

So it is that Jesus rests on the seventh day of the week, in death, in a borrowed grave. When John had objected to baptizing him, Jesus said, 'Let it be so now, for thus it is fitting for us to fulfil all righteousness' (3:15). If that was so then, it is doubly so now: Jesus' burial is the culmination of a life of righteousness, in which the wages of sin are imputed to the only man who ever lived completely without sin. Yet, even in his death he fulfils righteousness, as he rests in the grave on the seventh day of the week and 'sabbaths' in the rest of death prior to his appearing.

Matthew is careful to remind us of the reality of Jesus' burial, thereby preparing us for the reality of his resurrection. But in addition to the preparations made by Jesus' followers, he also reminds us that Pilate and the religious leaders who condemned Jesus are making their own plans. In case any of the disciples steal the body and claim that Jesus has risen, they make sure the grave will be watched under guard and protected by Pilate's seal. The whole authority of the Roman Empire is standing watch to make sure that no one will get into the grave. What they all fail to reckon with is the possibility that the person inside will get out!

FOR FURTHER STUDY

1. Matthew tells us that Judas sold Jesus for thirty pieces of silver. How does this detail reflect the following passages: Genesis 37:28; Exodus 21:32; Zechariah 11:12–13?
2. Jesus inaugurated a new meal for his people (26:26–29). What is the significance of the bread and the wine in this new supper?
3. Matthew tells us that in Gethsemane, Jesus began to be troubled and sorrowful (26:37). How did Matthew know this? What do these emotions tell us about Jesus?
4. How do the following passages shed light on Peter's denial: John 21:15–19; 1 Peter 1:5–7?
5. What was the significance of the torn curtain in 27:51? Compare this verse with Exodus 26:31–33 and Hebrews 10:19–22.

TO THINK ABOUT AND DISCUSS

1. How would you answer the question, 'Why did Jesus die?' Is more than one answer possible?
2. Does the account of Jesus in the garden of Gethsemane teach you something about the struggles of knowing and doing the will of God? Or should we handle these Scriptures differently?
3. B. B. Warfield says that 'Our Lord, though he died on the cross, yet died not of the cross but … of a broken heart.'[8] Do you agree?

14 Long live the King!

(28:1–15)

The cross is not the end; death does not have the last word in Matthew's Gospel. That honour belongs to resurrection and to the story of the empty tomb. At the beginning, Jesus emerged out of the darkness of the world's sin; at the end, he emerges out of the darkness of the grave.

The resurrection marks the triumph of the King. None of the Gospel narratives concludes with the burial of Jesus; they all testify to the reality of his resurrection. At one end of his life, his virginal conception attests supernatural beginnings; at the other, the resurrection attests a supernatural ending to his life in this world.

Resurrection (vv. 1–15)

Matthew concludes his story in three ways: with the

narrative of initial events at the grave, responses on the part of the Jewish leaders and Jesus' final commissioning of his disciples.

The resurrection represents the greatest revelation of God's plan of salvation in history. We believe in the resurrection as a doctrine of faith because we accept it as a fact of history. We believe in the eyewitness testimonies of those who saw the living Christ after he had been crucified, dead and buried.

Yet it remains true that no one actually saw the body of Jesus Christ coming to life in the silence of the tomb. The nineteenth-century American pastor T. V. Moore recognized the significance of this when he asked, 'Why did not Christ rise in the presence of a crowd?'[1] After all, Christ's death and ascension were public spectacles, which many people were present to witness. Yet the moment of resurrection was essentially private and hidden. There was no public display of life entering into the dead body of Jesus. Why did he not rise in the presence of a crowd?

The answer Moore himself supplies is that a secret resurrection places us all on the same level. No one is put at any advantage. All must take this doctrine on the basis of faith. The women must trust the angels; the disciples must trust the women; we must trust the disciples. We operate every day with the principle that truth may be established on the testimony of eyewitnesses. We punish criminals even when we did not see the crime being committed, precisely because the evidence gives away the truth of the matter.

So how does Matthew establish the fact of the resurrection for us?

First, the women come early to the grave of Jesus (v. 1). They, too, rested on the Sabbath day, and now they come to the grave early in the morning of the first day of the week. Their devotion to Jesus is explicitly highlighted by Matthew. They had lingered at both the cross and the grave; now they come early to see the tomb.

Second, the women encounter an angel (v. 2). The miraculous opening of the tomb is unexpected for the women, but not for the readers of Matthew's Gospel. After all, as early as Matthew 1:20 angels appear to announce the birth of Jesus. According to Matthew, it was the angel who rolled the stone from the entrance to the tomb, caused the Roman soldiers to panic and assured the women that Jesus had risen. This announcement from heaven contains a commission to the women to report the facts of Jesus' resurrection to the disciples. The angel also corroborates Jesus' statement that he will precede them into Galilee (26:32).

> False witnesses secured Jesus' death; false witnesses now try to conceal his resurrection.

Third, the women's joy at this news turns to worship as they encounter the living Jesus on the way and are greeted by him (v. 9). They respond to his greeting by prostrating themselves before him in worship. Jesus commissions them to continue on their journey and tell the disciples.

These three events together confirm the faith of the women, and subsequently that of the disciples, in the fact of the resurrection of Jesus. Matthew's Jesus is a living Jesus.

Meanwhile, the Jewish leaders, on their part, are at a loss (vv. 11–15). All they can do is concoct a story to cover the reality of the situation. Jesus has risen, but they spread the rumour that the disciples have stolen the body. That is a dangerous gamble, because the theft of the body would implicate them in not having guarded the tomb. False witnesses secured Jesus' death; false witnesses now try to conceal his resurrection.

The risen Jesus has triumphed! He now comes before us as the true King, with all authority in the universe, the sovereign of his kingdom and head of his church, which he sends into the world to continue the mission he began.

FOR FURTHER STUDY

1. According to 1 Timothy 3:16, Jesus was 'seen by angels'. What references to angels do we find in Matthew's Gospel?
2. In 28:9, women worship Jesus. What other reference to worship do we find in this chapter? Is Jesus a fitting object of worship?
3. According to 1 Corinthians 15:12–19, how vital is belief in the resurrection of Jesus?

TO THINK ABOUT AND DISCUSS

1. Why did Jesus not rise from the dead publicly?
2. Why do you think Matthew tells us of the plans of Jesus' enemies to contradict the story of the resurrection?

15 The King appoints ambassadors

(28:16–20)

The closing verses of Matthew's Gospel are often referred to as the 'Great Commission', a passage in which Jesus gives the church its 'marching orders'. While that is undoubtedly true, it is possible to read these verses simply as a conclusion to Matthew's Gospel in which some of the dominant themes of the Gospel are brought before us again.[1] Consider, for example, the following themes of this passage:

First, we see the theme of the *mountain*, to which the eleven disciples come (v. 16). The great sermon of chapters 5–7 was bracketed by references to the mountain (5:1; 8:1). For Jesus, the mountain was a place of solitude (14:23) as well as a place to meet the crowds (15:29–30). It was on a mountain that he was transfigured (17:1). Mountains are also referred to in connection with temptation (4:8), faith (17:20; 21:21) and security (24:16). This theme links the Gospel back to the theophany of Sinai in the Book of Exodus.

Second, we see the theme of *worship*, which is offered to Jesus on this occasion by the eleven (v. 17). Jesus has been the object of worship throughout this Gospel: by the wise men (2:2,11), by the disciples in the boat (14:33) and by the women after the resurrection (28:9). The devil tried to get Jesus to worship him (4:9), the response to which was that there is only one object of worship—the God of the Bible (4:10). Matthew wants us to learn that there is no incongruity between worshipping that one true God and offering our worship to Jesus. Worship Jesus of *is* worship of God.

Third, we see the theme of *faith*—or rather, perhaps, the theme of doubt (v. 17). 'Some doubted,' says Matthew, even in the presence of the risen Christ! Yet a remarkable thing has been going on in this Gospel. Jesus has found great faith in his ministry on the part of the Roman centurion (8:10), the friends of the paralytic (9:2), the woman with the discharge of blood (9:22) and the Canaanite woman (15:28). In many ways, these have been surprising discoveries of remarkable faith. Yet the disciples, who ought to have had great faith, are often spoken of as having little, as in the Sermon (6:30), in the boat (8:26), on the sea (14:31), by the shore (16:8) and after the transfiguration (17:20). Whether confronted by a storm, lack of bread or inability to cast out demons, the disciples are the doubters, while outside the apostolic circle Jesus often finds great faith.

Fourth, we see the theme of *authority* (v. 18). Jesus' claim to possess universal authority comes at the end of a Gospel where this has been a recurring theme. At the close of the Sermon on the Mount, it is recognized that Jesus' teaching has been with authority (7:29). His authority over the natural elements is a source of marvel in 8:27, while his healing of the paralysed man causes the crowds to glorify God, who has given this kind of authority to men (9:7). Now, however, his claim is absolute: *all* authority is his, in heaven and on earth.

Fifth, we see the theme of *the nations* (v. 19). The whole world is to become the theatre of the church's work and mission. At the beginning of the Gospel, the nations came to Jesus in the persons of the wise men from the east; now, he sends his church into the nations. He has already predicted that many will come from all directions to recline at table with Abraham, Isaac and Jacob (8:11), which is another way of saying that the covenant blessing will be universalized. By Jesus' interaction with a soldier of the Empire and a woman of Canaan, we have been prepared for this indication of a mission that will extend beyond the borders of ancient Israel.

Sixth, we see the theme of *discipleship* (v. 19). The church is to make disciples. She is not merely to evangelize and make converts, but to teach and make disciples. Jesus chose twelve to be apostles. He makes apostles. All apostles are disciples. But not all disciples are apostles—Joseph of Arimathea is called a disciple in 27:57. We make disciples as we preach the gospel and present men and women with the claims of Christ on their lives. We have learned that the nature of discipleship is to be like the Master (10:25) and to belong to the family of Jesus (12:49).

Seventh, we see the theme of *baptism* (v. 19). The reference to baptism links back to Jesus' own baptism in chapter 3 as well as to the claim of John that Jesus would baptize with the Holy Spirit (3:11). Although Jesus himself never baptizes with water in the Gospel narratives, he commissions his church to administer baptism in the communities of disciples. Some see baptism as a sign of God's covenant promise, as circumcision was in the Old Testament, and believe they have a warrant to baptize covenant children brought up within the community of disciples. Others see baptism as a sign of personal faith, and believe that baptism ought to be administered only to those who profess themselves to be disciples. Given the few references to baptism in the New Testament, it has proved a highly controversial subject in the history of the church. However, for both groups seeking to apply the terms of the Great Commission, baptism is a foundational, primary and initiatory rite of discipleship.

Eighth, the theme of the *Trinity* (v. 19). Baptism is 'into the name of God'. Explicitly, it is into one name ('the name of'), but that one name is three: Father, Son and Holy Spirit. Aspects of the Trinity have already been introduced through this Gospel: the child Jesus is God with us (1:23); the baptism of Jesus is clearly a Trinitarian event, as the Father speaks, the Son is baptized and the Spirit descends (3:13–17); the Holy Spirit whom Jesus gives is the Spirit of the Father (10:20); and outright rejection of Jesus constitutes blasphemy against the Holy Spirit (12:31).

Ninth, the theme of *teaching* (v. 20). Disciples are made by teaching and are nurtured by teaching. In Matthew's Gospel,

Jesus is the Moses-like prophet, whose discourses and blocks of teaching form a major part of the structure of the book. The church is to teach the things that Jesus has already taught. It is not surprising, therefore, to find echoes of Jesus' teaching pervading the New Testament. The words which God gave his Messiah continue in his children (Isa. 59:21).

Tenth, the theme of God's *presence* with his people (v. 20). At the outset of the Gospel, Jesus was named 'Immanuel', God with us (1:23), and he promises in the course of the Gospel narrative that even where two people gather in his name he is there (18:20). Now the presence of God in Christ by the Holy Spirit is promised to the commissioned church.

In all of this, therefore, the Great Commission summarizes the themes of the Gospel for us. More fundamentally still, the Great Commission concludes the Gospel of the Son of Abraham, to whom God originally promised that, by leaving his father's house, all the nations would be blessed (Gen. 12:1–3). Abraham's greatest Son has now come and he conveys blessing; the recipients of that blessing are to be the means by which it will be carried into the nations.[2]

Great Commission or Great Covenant?

As Matthew winds up his story, he does remind us that there is a commission to the church, as there is, arguably, in all four Gospels (see Mark 16:15; Luke 24:47; John 20:21). The gospel story is a motivating story. But God's purpose exists before God's church. It is *through* the church that God *fulfils* his purpose, not just *to* the church that he *announces* it.

In fact, given the heavy Old Testament influence on

Matthew's Gospel, it would not be going too far to see the Great Commission as deliberately set in the form of a covenant, which contains three elements:

First, the King of the church identifies himself. King Jesus has authority over the heavens and over the nations. The one who sends his church out with the message of saving grace is the one who stands supreme over the circle of the universe.

Second, the King of the church gives specific tasks to his covenant people. As they go, they are to disciple, by baptizing and teaching. They are to preach no new, original message, but the message which Christ himself has given to them.

Third, the King of the church makes promises conditional on obedience to his command. Can we claim the promise of his presence if we are not going into all the world with the gospel? This is the relationship he has with us, one in which he promises to work out his purpose through us, and accompany us on that great missionary task.

FOR FURTHER STUDY

1. How does the Great Commission of 28:19–20 compare or contrast with the call of Abraham in Genesis 12:1–3?
2. Paul uses the image of an 'ambassador' to describe his ministry in 2 Corinthians 5:20. What are some of the implications of this metaphor?

TO THINK ABOUT AND DISCUSS

1. How should the church implement the Great Commission today?
2. How is Jesus 'with us always'?

Table of Old Testament citations in Matthew's Gospel

The following table lists the formal quotations of, and references to, Old Testament passages that Matthew either simply cites or expressly tells us are fulfilled in the life of Christ. It does not take into account the 100 or so allusions to the Old Testament. For example, each use of the title Son of Man is an Old Testament allusion, as are the numerous references to Elijah.

1:23	Isa. 7:14	Virgin conception
2:6	Micah 5:2	Birth in Bethlehem
2:15	Hosea 11:1	Called out of Egypt
2:18	Jer. 31:15	Rachel weeping
2:23	Judg. 13:7; 16:17; Zech. 3:8; 6:12; Isa. 4:2	Called a Nazarene
3:3	Isa. 40:3	Preparing the way of the Lord
4:4	Deut. 8:3	Bread alone
4:5	Ps. 91:11	Angels looking after you
4:7	Deut. 6:16	Testing the Lord
4:10	Deut. 6:13	Worship the Lord only
4:15–16	Isa. 9:1–2	Light in darkness
5:21	Exod. 20:13; Deut. 5:17	Sixth commandment
5:27	Exod. 20:14; Deut. 5:18	Seventh commandment
5:31	Deut. 24:1	Divorce
5:38	Exod. 21:24; Lev. 24:20	An eye for an eye

5:43	Lev. 19:2,18	Love your neighbour
8:17	Isa. 53:4	He took our illnesses
9:13	Hosea 6:6	God desires mercy, not sacrifice
11:10	Mal. 3:1	God sends his messenger
12:7	Hosea 6:6	God desires mercy, not sacrifice
12:17–21	Isa. 42:1–4	Behold, my servant
13:14–15	Isa. 6:9–10	You will hear but not understand
13:35	Ps. 78:2	I will speak in parables
15:4	Exod. 20:12; 21:17; Deut. 5:16	Fifth commandment
15:8–9	Isa. 29:13	Honouring God with the lips, not the heart
19:4–5	Gen. 2:24	He made them male and female
19:18–19	Exod. 20:12–16; Lev. 19:18; Deut. 5:16–20	Citations of various commandments
21:5	Zech. 9:9	Entrance of the King on a donkey
21:9	Ps. 118:26	Blessed is he who comes
21:13	Isa. 56:7; Jer. 7:11	The house of God a den of robbers
21:16	Ps. 8:2	Praise from the lips of babes
21:42	Ps. 118:22–23	The stone the builders rejected
22:32	Exod. 3:6	The God of Abraham, Isaac and Jacob
22:37	Deut. 6:4–5	The first great commandment
22:44	Ps. 110:1	At God's right hand
23:39	Ps. 118:26	Blessed is he who comes
26:31	Zech.13:7	The smiting of the shepherd
27:9–10	Zech. 11:12–13 (and Jer. 19?)	The potter's field

Further reading

Commentaries and studies

J. M. Boice, *The Gospel of Matthew*, 1: *The King and His Kingdom (Matthew 1–17)* and 2: *The Triumph of the King (Matthew 18–28)*, (Grand Rapids: Baker Books, 2006).

R.T. France, *The Gospel of Matthew* (The New International Commentary on the New Testament; Grand Rapids, MI: Eerdmans, 2007).

D. Jackman and W. Philip, *Teaching Matthew: Unlocking the Gospel of Matthew for the Expositor* (London: Proclamation Trust/Fearn: Christian Focus Publications, 2003).

Craig S. Keener, *A Commentary on the Gospel of Matthew* (Grand Rapids, MI: Eerdmans, 1999).

J. Legg, *The King and his Kingdom: Matthew Simply Explained* (Welwyn Commentary Series; Darlington: Evangelical Press, 2004).

J. C. Ryle, *Expository Thoughts on Matthew* (Edinburgh: Banner of Truth, 1986).

D. L. Turner, *Matthew* (Baker Exegetical Commentary on the New Testament; Grand Rapids, MI: Baker Academic, 2008).

S. Westerholm, *Understanding Matthew: The Early Christian Worldview of the First Gospel* (Grand Rapids, MI: Baker Academic, 2006).

A. I. Wilson, *When Will These Things Happen? A Study of Jesus as Judge in Matthew 21–25* (Carlisle: Paternoster Biblical Monographs, 2004).

Reference and general works

G. K. Beale and D. A. Carson (eds.), *Commentary on the New Testament use of the Old Testament* (Grand Rapids, MI: Baker Books/Nottingham: Apollos, 2007).

C. L. Blomberg, *Jesus and the Gospels: An Introduction and Survey* (Leicester: Apollos, 1997).

D. A. Carson and D. J. Moo, *An Introduction to the New Testament* (Grand Rapids, MI: Zondervan, 2005).

S. Gathercole, *The Pre-Existent Son* (Grand Rapids, MI: Eerdmans, 2006).

D. G. Reid (ed.), *The IVP Dictionary of the New Testament: A One-Volume Compendium of Contemporary Biblical Scholarship* (Leicester: IVP, 2004).

Endnotes

Background and summary

1 Gerd Theissen, *The New Testament* (London: T & T Clark, 2003), p. 105.

2 Craig S. Keener, *A Commentary on the Gospel of Matthew* (Grand Rapids, MI: Eerdmans, 1999), p. 23.

3 Eusebius, *Ecclesiastical History*, 3.39; accessed on 12 September 2007 from the online edition of Eusebius at http://www.newadvent.org/fathers/250103.htm.

Chapter 1

1 Phil Ryken, *He Speaks to Me Everywhere* (Phillipsburg, NJ: P&R, 2004), p. 144.

2 Ibid. p. 145.

Chapter 2

1 Merrill Tenney, *New Testament Survey* (Grand Rapids, MI: Eerdmans, 1961), p. 110.

2 Robert Letham, *The Holy Trinity: In Scripture, History, Theology and Worship* (Phillipsburg, NJ: P&R, 2004), p. 391.

Chapter 3

1 J. R. W. Stott, *The Message of the Sermon on the Mount* (Leicester: IVP, 1978), p. 33.

2 Ibid. p. 104.

3 See Stott's discussion in *Sermon on the Mount*, pp. 105–114.

4 Westminster Larger Catechism, Q. 187.

Chapter 4

1 S. Gathercole, *The Pre-Existent Son* (Grand Rapids, MI: Eerdmans, 2006), p. 153.

2 See Gathercole, *Pre-Existent Son*, ch. 6, where he discusses the 'I have come' sayings in the Synoptic Gospels; he says that their form and parallels 'point toward preexistence' as well as towards 'a deliberate action in coming with a purpose' (p. 170).

Chapter 5

1 C. J. H. Wright, 'Covenant: God's Mission through God's People', in J. A. Grant and A. I. Wilson (eds), *The God of Covenant* (Leicester: Apollos, 2005), p. 61.

Chapter 6

1 B. B. Warfield, 'The Emotional Life of our Lord', in *The Person and Work of Christ* (Philadelphia: P&R, 1980), p. 96.

2 Ibid. p. 99.

3 John MacArthur, *The MacArthur New Testament Commentary: Matthew 8–15* (Chicago: Moody Press, 1987), p. 431.

4 St John Chrysostom, Homily LIII on Matthew, from *Nicene and Post-Nicene Fathers*, series I, vol. X , Roger Pearse, *The Fathers of the Church in English Translation* (CD-ROM, 2004).

5 G. Vos, *The Self-Disclosure of Jesus* (New York: George H. Doran, 1926), p. 181.

Chapter 8

1 John Piper, *What Jesus Demands from the World* (Wheaton: Crossway Books, 2006), p. 71.

Chapter 9

1 John MacArthur, *On Divorce: Matthew 19:1–12*, (John MacArthur's Bible Studies; Chicago: Moody Press, 1985), p. 7.

2 J. M. Boice, *The Gospel of Matthew*, ii: *The Triumph of the King (Matthew 18–28)* (Grand Rapids: Baker Books, 2006), p. 403.

3 For further reading on this theme, including good discussion of this passage, see Stephen Clark, *Putting Asunder: Divorce and Remarriage in Biblical and Pastoral Perspective* (Bryntirion: Bryntirion Press, 1999).

Chapter 10

1 C. L. Blomberg, *Jesus and the Gospels: An Introduction and Survey* (Leicester: Apollos, 1997), p. 314.

2 A. I. Wilson, *When Will These Things Happen? A Study of Jesus as Judge in Matthew 21–25* (Carlisle: Paternoster Biblical Monographs, 2004), p. 91.

3 Ibid. p. 93.

4 'There is every indication that Jesus intended his entry to be a prophetic act, in the tradition of the OT prophets …' (Ibid. p. 89).

Chapter 11

1 See Wilson, *When Will These Things Happen?*, pp. 96–97 for a discussion on the importance of Zechariah to this section of Matthew.

2 Matthew Henry on Matthew 21:27, *Commentary on the Whole Bible*, v.

3 Wilson, *When Will These Things Happen?*, p. 102.

Chapter 12

1 *Collected Writings of John Murray*, ii (Edinburgh: Banner of Truth, 1977), p. 39.

2 For further discussion on these themes, see Wilson, *When Will These Things Happen?*, pp. 238–247.

Chapter 13

1 R.A. Finlayson, *The Cross in the Experience of our Lord* (London: Parry Jackman, n.d.), p. 53.

2 B. B. Warfield, *The Person and Work of Christ* (Phillipsburg, NJ: P&R, 1980), p. 132.

3 Hugh Martin, *The Shadow of Calvary* (Edinburgh: Lyon & Gemmell, 1875), p. 28.

4 D. L. Bock, *Blasphemy and Exaltation in Judaism: The Charge against Jesus in Mark 14:53–65* (Grand Rapids: Baker Books, 2000), p. 236.

5 A. Wroe, *Pilate: The Biography of an Invented Man* (London: Vintage, 2000), p. 214.

6 See, for example, Boice, *Gospel of Matthew*, ii, p. 601.

7 Wroe, *Pilate*, p. 238.

8 Warfield, *Person and Work of Christ*, p. 133.

Chapter 14

1 T. V. Moore, *The Last Days of Jesus* (Edinburgh: Banner of Truth, 1981), p. 18.

Chapter 15

1 For this insight I am particularly indebted to D. W. Chapman, 'The Great Commission as the Conclusion of Matthew's Gospel', in R. A. Peterson and S. M. Lucas (eds), *All for Jesus: A Celebration of the 50th Anniversary of Covenant Theological Seminary* (Mentor: Fearn, 2006), pp. 85–101.

2 For an excellent discussion of the call of Abraham as the original Great Commission, and the connection between Genesis 12 and Matthew 28, see C. J. H. Wright, *The Mission of God* (Leicester: IVP, 2006), especially ch. 6.

About Day One:

Day One's threefold commitment:

- To be faithful to the Bible, God's inerrant, infallible Word;
- To be relevant to our modern generation;
- To be excellent in our publication standards.

I continue to be thankful for the publications of Day One. They are biblical; they have sound theology; and they are relative to the issues at hand. The material is condensed and manageable while, at the same time, being complete—a challenging balance to find. We are happy in our ministry to make use of these excellent publications.

JOHN MACARTHUR, PASTOR-TEACHER, GRACE COMMUNITY CHURCH, CALIFORNIA

It is a great encouragement to see Day One making such excellent progress. Their publications are always biblical, accessible and attractively produced, with no compromise on quality. Long may their progress continue and increase!

JOHN BLANCHARD, AUTHOR, EVANGELIST AND APOLOGIST

Visit our website for more information and to request a free catalogue of our books.

www.dayone.co.uk

Opening up series

Title	Author	ISBN
Opening up 1 Corinthians	Derek Prime	978–1–84625–004–0
Opening up 1 Thessalonians	Tim Shenton	978–1–84625–031–6
Opening up 1 Timothy	Simon J Robinson	978–1–903087–69–5
Opening up 2 & 3 John	Terence Peter Crosby	978–1–84625–023–1
Opening up 2 Peter	Clive Anderson	978–1–84625–077–4
Opening up 2 Thessalonians (in preparation)	Ian McNaughton	978–1–84625–117–7
Opening up 2 Timothy	Peter Williams	978–1–84625–065–1
Opening up Amos	Michael Bentley	978–1–84625–041–5
Opening up Colossians & Philemon	Ian McNaughton	978–1–84625–016–3
Opening up Ecclesiastes	Jim Winter	978–1–903087–86–2
Opening up Exodus	Iain D Campbell	978–1–84625–029–3
Opening up Ezekiel's visions	Peter Jeffery	978–1–903087–66–4
Opening up Ezra	Peter Williams	978–1–84625–022–4
Opening up Hebrews	Philip Hacking	978–1–84625–042–2
Opening up Jonah	Paul Mackrell	978–1–84625–080–4

Opening up Joshua (in preparation)	Roger Ellsworth	978–1–84625–118–4
Opening up Judges	Simon J Robinson	978–1–84625–043–9
Opening up Luke's Gospel	Gavin Childress	978–1–84625–030–9
Opening up Malachi	Roger Ellsworth	978–1–84625–033–0
Opening up Matthew	Iain D Campbell	978–1–84625–116–0
Opening up Nahum	Clive Anderson	978–1–903087–74–9
Opening up Philippians	Roger Ellsworth	978–1–903087–64–0
Opening up Proverbs	Jim Newheiser	978–1–84625–110–8
Opening up Psalms	Roger Ellsworth	978–1–84625–005–7
Opening up Ruth	Jonathan Prime	978–1–84625–067–5
Opening up Titus	David Campbell	978–1–84625–079–8
Opening up Zephaniah	Michael Bentley	978–1–84625–111–5